Julian Beck

Prometheus

The Archaeology of Sleep

TWO PLAYS

Fast Books

Fast Books are edited and published by Michael Smith
P. O. Box 1268, Silverton, OR 97381
info@fastbookspress.com

ISBN 978-0-9982793-9-8

CONTENTS

PROMETHEUS

Edited by Tom Walker
assistant editor Robert Hieger

INTRODUCTION
by Tom Walker

The Living Theatre began to create *Prometheus* in the summer of 1977. The group had been touring without stop for a year through Italy, Belgium, France, Spain, Portugal, and Switzerland. Finally enough money had been earned to rent two apartments and settle down in Rome to start new work.

The creation of *Prometheus* was a significant departure for the company because it was the first time in seven years that The Living Theatre had decided to create a play expressly for the indoor legitimate theatre space. In 1970 the group had taken the step of leaving established theatre in order to take theatre to people who never went to the bourgeois theatre. In Brazil, then the United States, and finally in Italy, The Living Theatre performed in schools, factories, prisons, insane asylums, and in streets and town squares. Except for the occasional festival, the group depended on grants and alternative financial support other than the box office.

By the end of 1976, after half a year of Italian touring with *The Money Tower, Six Public Acts,* and *Seven Meditations on Political Sado-Masochism*, the group found itself in Naples, penniless. The decision was made to take *Seven Meditations* to regular performance venues. We began with local anarchist sponsors in the Massa Carrara area of Tuscany and proceeded on to a European tour with the intent to make enough money to settle down to create a new work for that theatre system abandoned years before. We would still perform in the streets, but the box office would once again become the principal support for The Living Theatre.

Seven Meditations, which had been the workhorse in the repertoire, had no set, few lights, no light cues, and was an intensely ritualistic show. *Prometheus* was to be a total theatre

3

creation with a large set, extensive lighting, and many costumes. The fifteen or so members of the group began to meet for long hours every day to discuss what a play on the subject of Prometheus would be.

The Prometheus myth had long been on Julian Beck's mind. Once in high school when a teacher asked who he wanted to be when he grew up, Julian replied, "I want to be Prometheus." The idea of stealing the power of the gods, of freedom for humankind, of an end to punishment, had been a central theme throughout The Living Theatre's work since the beginning.

Texts were consulted. The Aeschylus play was studied. One September afternoon everyone trooped off to the Baths of Caracalla to read together Shelley's "Prometheus Unbound" amid the ruins where he had written much of the poem. The films of Jean Cocteau were studied as well, providing a style for our first act.

The first act would be a basic retelling of the myth, an introduction of themes. People chose their characters. Julian would be Zeus, Judith, Io. With advice from Judith, I chose The Furies; it seemed appropriate, for I was sometimes given to rages in those days. This choice might serve as a way to get on top of it; there would certainly be some energy for the role. Carlo Altomare, our musician, chose Orpheus.

People chose characters who were close to the Prometheus myth: for example, Pandora, who also dares to disobey the gods. Some actors chose a character based on the inanimate. For example, Ilion Troya chose to represent Fire, the energy stolen by Prometheus. Rain House, who had long seen himself as an androgyne, chose Narcissus.

After many meetings, Julian wove a text together based on our sources, the characters chosen, our discussions, and our desire for audience participation; it was a text based on who and what The Living Theatre was at that particular point in its development, mixed with the magic of theatre. Julian

Devising *Prometheus*, Rome, 1977. Clockwise from left front: Ilion Troya, Carol Westernik, Tom Walker, Julian Beck, Judith Malina.

also used parts of poems he had already written before the work on *Prometheus*. Parts of his *Songs of the Revolution* are incorporated into the introductory Hell Cantata. A section of his poem cycle *Daily Light, Daily Speech, Daily Life* becomes Orpheus's first lines. He also drew on his knowledge of many of his favorite writers. In the final scene in Act I, The Fire Theft, Orpheus sings, "To curve of shore, to bend of bay..." alluding to the opening of *Finnegans Wake*. An appendix lists Julian's sources as he listed them in the program.

This first act arrived with the new year. Now Julian began a second act which came from him alone. He spent many hours in the tiny archive room of the Via Gaeta apartment at his small desk. When he presented the second act to us it was fully formed.

All of our first-act characters had been transformed and dropped down on top of the events of the Russian Revolution. And the ultimate act of audience participation was his coup de théâtre: to invite and rehearse audience members to storm the Winter Palace with us in the play.

It is important to realize the Italian political atmosphere of the time to understand the symbolism for Julian of using the Russian Revolution as a form for his work about Prometheus. The Living Theatre had returned to Italy in the mid-'70s as the country was being rocked by the struggles of the Red Brigades on the far left, the ultra-fascist groups on the far right, the corrupt Christian Democratic party, which had held onto power since World War II, the Mafia, and the Italian Communist Party, which was the most independent and successful of all the western European communist parties. Add into this a lively anarchist tradition with many active groups, a pacifist movement, and a climate of bomb explosions and political assassinations, and you have a provocative context in which to critique individual freedom and the, among many, venerated legend of the Russian Revolution. Many of our sponsors were Italian Communists, and it is a tribute to their flexibility that they were objective and supportive of Julian's critical portrait of Lenin and the Bolsheviks. In any case, Julian knew that our audiences would be highly conversant with his subject matter. His first act presented the myth; his second act presented how that myth informed the issues of the day.

In June 1978 we finally began rehearsals for the play. Julian secured a contract to open *Prometheus* in Rome in September at the Teatro Argentina, with an anteprima in Prato, the industrial city near Florence. We rehearsed through the hot summer in a small theatre lent to us near St. Peter's. Sometimes we would go outside to the grounds surrounding the Castello Sant' Angelo for more space. Pope Paul VI died; a new pope was chosen; he died; and so it went amid pomp and heat, and we rehearsed.

Stefan Schulberg, who was originally to play Prometheus, wanted to write his own text in Act I. He and Julian argued and then seemed to work out their disagreements, but Stefan decided to depart nonetheless. He and his companion, Antonia Masulli, and their six-month-old son, Satya, were to be away from the company for two years, concentrating on Satya's development and other projects. Hanon Reznikov took over the role of Prometheus.

Paul Broom, who was to play Hephaestus, was also our technical chief. He made several experiments in the Sant' Angelo gardens with metal pipe. One day in late August, when we were rehearsing in the Teatro Valle, Julian called in workmen skilled in erecting the metal scaffolding for the restoration of Italy's old buildings. In a few hours they had constructed two towers with a bridge across the proscenium between them, and two metal ladders rising diagonally from the base of the towers to the center of the bridge. A rock of many pipes for Prometheus was positioned at the center of the bridge. A pyramid for Zeus was constructed upstage. The workmen were so pleased with what they had created, unlike anything they had ever done, that photographs of them were taken in front of their handiwork. We were left with this mountain of metal to take apart, construct, and transport. It took about six hours to build and two hours to take down, with six to eight people working. The connection of the first pipes to form the bridge was quite dangerous. A myriad of small props were made. There were some thirty costumes. Carlo used many musical instruments and machines. The scenography also called for several small platforms, a hexagonal tunnel of metal and wood, projection screens, giant maps, and a snow machine. All of this would move about Italy and Europe in a very large truck. The actors loaded the truck.

In early September we moved to Prato for final rehearsals. Julian set about designing more than 300 light cues. Julian presented his idea for the third act with only a few days left before the opening. The proposal seemed too much to realize in the short time we had left; after some experimentation, Julian threw the idea out (it is printed as an appendix). He opted instead for the performers to leave the theatre at the end, inviting the audience to come with them, and proceed to the nearest prison for a vigil in the name of the end of punishment, the Promethean theme. Deceptively simple, the idea seemed to catch the spirit of the moment: to leave the bourgeois theatre once again for a direct action in the street. We all agreed with the plan; it was a quick solution, a dramatic one, and we ended up performing it all over Europe for the next year.

When the play opened on September 25th, it ran to almost four hours. Several cuts would eventually keep it to three hours. The audience reception and participation was enthusiastic. For the third-act vigil we processed to the nearby headquarters of the carabinieri where there was a holding prison. The police forced us to move after about fifteen minutes. The vigil for the following two nights was held in front of the old castle in the middle of town, which had once been a prison as well. Hundreds of members of the audience joined in the vigils.

The next week in Rome, the first night vigil was forbidden due to riots that had occurred in the city that day, but we were able to hold the vigil outside the Regina Coeli prison during the rest of the run. One night the whole company was taken into the nearest precinct for identification. The first night audience at the Teatro Argentina included Alberto Moravia and Renata Nicolini, the director of culture for Rome, who became a terrorist in the Act II assault on the Winter Palace. The play was a success.

The Living Theatre then embarked on a tour that took *Prometheus* to Ireland, France, Belgium, and Luxembourg. In Lille we performed in the Salle Roger Salengro, where the Second International had been held in the last century. After a holiday break, 1979 saw *Prometheus* travel through eleven Italian cities. Some were one-night stands, difficult with such a large set. In Ferrara after the vigil, the crowd on leaving the local prison became somewhat raucous. The police were not amused. We had been getting permission ahead of time for each vigil. But after Ferrara, permission began to be denied. On April 7th there had been massive arrests across Italy of many people of supposed leftist sympathies who were thought to be the above-ground support for the Red Brigades. After Ferrara, we would announce the vigil, then announce its prohibition by the authorities, listing all the places where the vigil had already taken place. There would be sustained applause.

The last performances of *Prometheus,* after three weeks in London at the Round House, were in Greece in the fall. The reception was rapturous, first in Salonika and then in Piraeus. *Prometheus* had been performed seventy-five times, before more than 30,000 spectators (see Appendix). Twenty years later it is still discussed in Italian theatre circles.

Julian Beck continued to write about Prometheus. His second volume of meditations on the theatre, *Theandric* (after *The Life of the Theatre,* 1972), has several references to Prometheus. In "Aphorisms" from that book, he writes: "Passivity, that's the danger. It is what Prometheus never experienced."

And further:

PROMETHEUS
He held the glass upside down and, arm extended like the branch of a tree bit by bit and more and more weighted by snow, let it slowly descend until the mosquito was trapped under it. Deftly sliding a postcard under the rim of the glass, careful not to injure the animal, she/he carries it to the door, opens it, releases the insect, steps back, closes the door, is unstung, and la zanzara is out of the way and alive.

In another section, remembering the high school student of long ago, he wrote:

9

PROMETHEUS

joyce modeled his life on dante, mann on goethe, and whom have you chosen, asked the high school teacher. prometheus, the young man murmured to himself, not loud enough for anyone to hear. he would have to hide it in a yarrow stalk, he would have to deceive it in order to unimprison the truth. dangerous ground. the cult of safety, the middle way, a middle-class cult, culture, an ultimate failure.

In his final play, *The Archaeology of Sleep* (1983), Julian wrote a character, Hanon (played by Hanon Reznikov), who in the multidream structure of the work recurrently dreams that he is playing the role of Prometheus, but this time in a movie. As the many subplots and dreams are woven together, the character and the playwright make their way toward a collective dream, the Promethean ideal of freedom from the nightmare of repressive authority.

Julian worked on many theatre pieces in The Living Theatre with Judith Malina, Hanon Reznikov, and the many members of the group who contributed action and text over the years. There were the plays of the '60s—*Mysteries and Smaller Pieces, Frankenstein,* and *Paradise Now;* and the plays of *The Legacy of Cain* cycle in the '70s—*The Money Tower, Seven Meditations, Six Public Acts*—and numerous street plays. However, *Prometheus* and *The Archaeology of Sleep* were most entirely Julian's. He devoted his life to the Promethean ideal. He thrust himself into every aspect of the realization of *Prometheus,* possessed and defined by the work. And even in *Archaeology,* he found himself still bound on that Promethean trip between wakefulness, sleep, and dream, searching his way toward the goal.

Editor's Note: The text of *Prometheus* is based on Julian Beck's typed working script. In this script he made many cuts in pen and in pencil, and wrote in many additions, corrections, and rearrangements of lines. The editor has included these changes in the final text, which was checked against audio tapes made of performances of the final version of the play (London, 1979). In 1984 Julian agreed that I undertake this task. He did not live to see its completion.   T.W.

CAST
(at The Round House, London, June 1979)

Mariarosa Arnosti – PANTHEA, TOLSTOYAN ANARCHO-PACIFIST

Carlo Altomare – ORPHEUS, VLADIMIR MAYAKOVSKY, SERGEI ESSENIN

Apollo Broom – HEPHAESTUS, BOLSHEVIK, KRONSTADT SAILOR

Toby Marshall – EROS, ANARCHIST BOLSHEVIK

Hanon Reznikov – PROMETHEUS, ALEXANDER BERKMAN, PIOTR KROPOTKIN

Ilion Troya – FIRE, BOLSHEVIK, TERRORIST, ALEXANDER ULYANOV, ANARCHIST, FATHER GAPON

Julian Beck – ZEUS, HERMES, OCEANUS, V. I. LENIN, LEO TROTSKY, CZAR ALEXANDER II

Tom Walker – THE FURIES, BOLSHEVIK, LEO KAMENEV, DEMOGORGON

Rain House – NARCISSUS, ANARCHIST

Judith Malina – IO, EMMA GOLDMAN

Mary Mary – HERA, EVE, LILITH, PROMETHEA, KRUPSKAYA, CZARINA

Imke Buchholz – METIS, BOLSHEVIK, ANARCHIST PRISONER, FEMINIST, CLARA ZETKIN

Carol Westernik – PANDORA, ANARCHIST, ISADORA DUNCAN

Text written and assembled by Julian Beck

Directed by Judith Malina & Julian Beck

Music by Carlo Altomare

Special Choreography by Jessica Sayre

Luminous sculptures by Toby Marshall

Setting by Julian Beck and Paul Broom

The company: back, Antonia Masulli, Stefan Schulberg, Tom Walker, Julian Beck, Judith Malina, Ilion Troya, Mariarosa Arnosti, Apollo Broom, Carol Westernik; middle, Rain House, Hanon Reznikov, Argento; front, Toby Marshall, Carlo Altomare, Mary Mary Krapf

Lighting designed by Julian Beck

Masks and Screens by Ilion Troya

Stage Manager: Ilana Abramovitch

Costumes executed by Mariarosa Arnosti and Carol Westemik

Music performed by Carlo Altomare, Jorg Fischer, and Toby Marshall

Technical Assistants – Argento, Jorg Fischer, Christian Vollmer

Lighting Technicians – Cristina Cibils, Ricardo Antonetti, Alfredo Gentile

13

SETTING

Two towers of metal scaffolding pipes support a narrow bridge-like span high above the front of the stage. A jagged cluster of short pipes in the center of the span is the promontory on which PROMETHEUS will be bound. It is reached by two metal ladders sloping diagonally inwards toward the crag from the feet of the towers.

Upstage is a tall pyramid of scaffolding with four horizontal levels. The shallow lowest level is, at the end of Act I, the home of FIRE in captivity. The second level, high enough to stand up in, is a heavily barred prison; the third level is the cramped lair of the FURIES. The summit is Olympus.

A Tunnel, octagonal in shape, leads offstage, upstage left. At stage right a tubular metal structure supports three platforms of different heights: one square, one trapezoidal, one octagonal. It is the Orpheum, the home of the creative, and it contains a variety of musical instruments and electronic equipment. On the octagon is the Dream Machine, made of metal and plastic.

PROMETHEUS

ACT I

PROMETHEUS THE FIREBRINGER
THE MYTHS

THE PROLOGUE IN THE THEATRE

As the audience enters, the actressors are sitting in various seats around the theatre—seats for which they have tickets—and firmly bound to them with black cords. The house lights are on, the stage dimly lit.

A tape sound is playing from the Orpheum as the public enters. A steady beat played on a slit drum continues without alteration. This steady beat is accompanied by a few recorded phrases spoken by the actressors during rehearsals. The words are repeated in loops so that we almost always hear the same phrase three times in a row. The tape lines and the lines recited by ORPHEUS *during The Prologue Onstage are collectively titled "The Breasts of Prometheus." The first voice is Judith Malina's.*

JUDITH MALINA'S VOICE
    No living thing to suffer pain
    the point is clear
    now how do you get through
    No living thing to suffer pain
    the point is clear
    now how do you get through
    No living thing to suffer pain
    the point is clear
    now how do you get through
    to all the people to understand this

CAROL WESTERNIK'S VOICE
What time is it please
can I look out
What time is it please
what time is it please
can I look out

CARLO ALTOMARE'S VOICE
There is a secret known to thee and to none else of living things.
There is a secret known to thee and to none else of living things.
There is a secret known to thee and to none else of living things.
(Shelley, "Prometheus Unbound")

This cycle is repeated by itself for about ten minutes. Then woven into it come other voices.

JULIAN BECK
What people whose lives are but a day possess already. The hot radiance of fire?
(Shelley, "Prometheus Unbound")

MARY MARY
Tear the veil.
(Shelley, "Prometheus Unbound")

JUDITH MALINA
The Age of Power is going to be over
That's it...

JULIAN BECK
The tele of dreams what fate ordained, interrupted by hidden sense of voices...
(Shelley, "Prometheus Unbound")

CAROL WESTERNIK
I have to find the connection

16

I have to find the connection

JULIAN BECK
  Various modes of prophecy

STEFAN SCHULBERG
  Prometheus
  Promeeeetheooooooooosss

JULIAN BECK
  Fire Fire Fire Fire Fire Fire

The Prologue in the Theatre lasts as long as it takes for the public to untie the actressors. As the actoresses are untied, they go one by one onto the stage.

The Prologue Onstage

The Hell Cantata

If another actoress is untied before Orpheus, *he or she unties* Orpheus, *who is the first of the actoresses to come on stage. He goes to the Orpheum and picks up on a drum the rhythm that has been playing on the tape. He turns down the tape; the rhythm changes from a slow regular single-note beat to a rapid beat of fluctuating timbre. Approxtmately every twenty seconds* Orpheus *speaks a phrase of poetry. Every other line contains either the word "living" or the word "fire" or related words. The phrases are an anthology gathered from the poems of poets of the so-called Beat Generation. These lines of poetry signal the actressors to move or freeze. Here follow* Orpheus's *cue lines, a continuation of "The Breasts Of Prometheus":*

Orpheus

    Living shadow voices
    Fire sets flame to nature
    Deep in each other's breathless living
    Burning like a …
    Living in metallic cities
    They were burning their own houses
    Blue veil over living
    … Living skin like a garment
    Fire against the …
    Living on hands and feet
    … with a thousand fires
    l wept in the land of the living
    Turn the pages of his burning books
    Kissing … of living …
    Madness triple fire
    Fire … the ground
    Change into fire
    Fires in the plain

As each actress is untied and approaches the stage, ORPHEUS *sings a number from 1 to 12. It is the number to which the actress must go in order that the pattern of movement proceed without conflicts. Thirteen points have been marked on the stage floor, and each actress moves from one point to another in such a way that no two actresses ever occupy the same point at the same time nor ever come into conflict with each other in occupying a point. Each actress has his or her own individual route through the thirteen points. No two routes are the same.*

The number 1 position, or Hot Spot, is in the center of the forefront of the stage. The movement of the actresses is improvised. They move when ORPHEUS *speaks a line containing the word "fire." They freeze—on the appropriate numerical point—when* ORPHEUS *speaks a phrase containing the word "living."*

There are five movements which all of the actresses must do at some point in the course of the action, at any point the actress selects to do them. There are the movements of

1) *Despair*

2) *The Making of Mudras*

3) *The Attica Prison Walk, hands clasped behind head*

4) *The Political Militant*

5) *a movement expressive of Paranoia, fast and jagged.*

As soon as each actress is untied he/she begins to whisper a phrase. He/she repeats this phrase throughout the duration of the Prologue.

HANON
  No change
  No peace no hope
  Yet I endure
  (Shelley, "Prometheus Unbound")

JULIAN
  It's been going for 10,000 years

I am pleading for the imagination as the solution.
(Julian Beck, "Songs of the Revolution," no. 79)

JUDITH
We want
to zap them
with holiness

TOBY
This is the song of rising flesh
This is the song
of new vibrations
(Julian Beck, "Songs of the Revolution," no. 57)

MARY MARY
We will assault
The culture
We will change the wind

ILION
Military firepower
It must be
Put out

TOM
It is 1968
I am a magic realist
I see the adorers of Che Guevara
(Julian Beck, "Revolution and Counter-revolution")

CAROL
What time is it?
wake up:
get rid of your watches!

PAUL
when the mind
lets go of violence
we will create new vessels

RAIN
if 1 have anything you want
take it
I'm free!

MARIAROSA
We want to anoint
your body and mine
with love

IMKE
it is time for everyone
to energize
and begin a voyage

When all of the actoresses have been freed by the public and are on stage, the lights in the theatre go down and lights on the stage brighten. The light on the Hot Spot intensifies. When each actoress moves into the Hot Spot he/she speaks his/her phrase out loud, with passion and intensity.

The combination of movement, phrases, and the phrases spoken by ORPHEUS *are an evocation of the past as exemplified by the culture of the 1960s.*

When the twelfth person speaks the twelfth phrase out loud ...

HANON
no change no pause no hope, yet I endure

... everyone falls to the ground and, making a humming sound, raises his/her head and trunk, supporting himself or herself on the palms of the hands and looking straight out at the audience.

CHORUS
We have to face
once again
all the issues
economic political
artistic

which have been
with the Living
since the very
beginning.

*The chorus is spoken in an extenuated rhythm. Over the voices of
everyone, one voice is heard, speaking clearly.*

JUDITH
We have to face
once again
all the issues
economic political
artistic
which have been
with The Living
Theatre
since the very
beginning.

(Julian Beck in *We The Living Theatre* by Julian Beck, Judith Malina, and
Aldo Rostagno)

*As soon as the chorus ends, the sound and movement becomes frenetic.
The next person to move into the Hot Spot is* MARY MARY.

MARY MARY
We will assault the culture
We will change
The wind.

JULIAN *(joins her on the word "wind" and cries out)*
Wind! Sweep over the fields!
Clean out the corridor

*As he comes out with the word "wind," everyone moves backward
upstage left, some rolling over, as if blown away, into the Tunnel.*

MARY MARY
Fresh rivers of air!

22

RAIN

Tear off my armor

TOM

Clean out my ears!
Let me hear!

Everyone, including ORPHEUS, *disappears, blown away, into the Tunnel. The lights dim down during the blowaway to blackout. The sound of the wind which came with the incantation, blowing away the rhythmic drum sound made by* ORPHEUS, *disappears also into a moment of silence. Then, in the dark, another sound emerges, low and musical.*

The House of the Creative

At the place where the spectators know the mouth of the Tunnel to be, a small white dot of light appears in the darkness. It is Panthea, who brings a primal light of wisdom out of the darkness. She speaks in Greek the first three depositions of Euclid's "Elements." She translates them into English. In this way we begin with the founder of our knowledge.

Panthea

Alpha: Semcion estin, ou mcros outhen
A point is that which has no parts.

Beta: Gramme de mekos aplates
A line is length without breadth.

Gamma: Grammes de perata semeia
The extremities of a line are points.

The dot of light becomes a line of light moving across the stage from the mouth of the Tunnel, dividing it in half. As Panthea reaches the center of the stage, a dim turquoise light illumines her dark figure moving, bending, pulling, turning: a woman pulling light out of the earth; as she reaches the other side of the stage, the sound of a human voice, Orpheus singing, begins to emerge from the Tunnel. The line of light is drawing him out. It pulls the luminous lyre he is playing. He emerges singing, and as he reaches the mouth of the Tunnel, Eros and Hephaestus—Feeling and Form—raise him on their shoulders and bear him across the stage as he sings. As the light grows gradually brighter, it is seen that Panthea is drawing him out of the Tunnel by a line which delineates the relation of mathematics to music. The theme is the emergence of the Past, coming up from the Underworld, out of Hell, singing, joyful, prepared to enter into poetry, passing from historical time which is strict and linear into mythic time, which is glowing and cyclic.

Orpheus
(*sings*)
hell gelb

clear yellow
clair
giallo di cromo scuro
amarillo cromo claro
jaune aurore
light
hell chromgelb
bianco di cina
blanco di plato
giallo di limone
theatre light
amarillo dorado
indian yellow
antimony yellow
arancio
lemon yellow
jaune de cadmium clair
more beautiful than **light**
are the words we have made to name it
the loud light of our mouths
(Julian Beck, "Daily Light Daily Speech Daily Life")

HEPHAESTUS
    ultramarine and acqua
    yellow and black and pale and hectic red
    if there is so much light in the world
    the form will have feeling

EROS
    the colors of love
    carmine lake
    vermillion
    terra naturale

EROS *with arrow poised, ready to fly, is about to strike* PANTHEA.
*She disarms him by asking the question which enlightens him as to
the meaning of his action.*

25

PANTHEA
why do you hunt?
what do you want to kill?
the total light we are seeking
begins in the ...

The music ORPHEUS *has been making changes with alarming brusqueness. A discordant chord. The lights change. The intense turquoise colors and gold are swept away by the sound of wind. The stage becomes ice blue, pale grey.*

ORPHEUS
(playing)
The scene represents a desolate landscape,
A great rock towers.
Enter Strength and Violence, Kratos ek Bia,
with the giant figure of
PROMETHEUS.

PROMETHEUS THE FIREBRINGER

During his speech, PROMETHEUS *is taken to the Promontory by* HEPHAESTUS.

PROMETHEUS
We have come to the end of the earth.
The Scythian Pale.
A vast and Ghastly Land.
And now, Hcphaestus, carry out the order given to you by my father.
Clamp this law-wrecker to a sky-piercing crag with unbreakable chains.
It was your treasure he stole, flashing fire, source of all arts, and gave to mortal creatures.
This is his offense, for which he must pay the gods the penalty until he be taught to bear and to like the sovereignty of Zeus and quit playing the lover of mankind.

HEPHAESTUS
Lofty-minded son of Themis
for you the will of Zeus is now accomplished.
In you there is nothing to stand in its way.
But for me—I cannot nerve myself to violently bind a kindred god here on this wintry cliff.
And yet I must, heart or no heart, this I must do. Against my will, no less than yours,
I fasten you with brazen bonds no hand can loose here to this desolate peak.
Here you will hear no human voice.
Here you will sec no mortal form.
Each changing hour will bring successive pain, and no man born will set you free.

PROMETHEUS
This is what you get for being kind to people.

HEPHAESTUS

A god who would not bow to the god's anger.
You gave to those who die greater power than they deserve.
For that you will keep watch on this joyless rock.
Erect, unsleeping, your knee unbending,
Many a groan and cry you will utter, all useless.
For the mind of Zeus is hard to soften with prayer, and
everyone is harsh who comes to power.

THE POET AND PROMETHEUS

The Chariot of Hours: ORPHEUS. *A mad percussion piece. Tin-like.*
Cocteau-like. Tin Cocteau. EROS, HEPHAESTUS, *and* PANTHEA *join*
the playing. Sound interspersed with conch shells, horns, saxophone.
EROS's *and* HEPHAESTUS's *movements are rapid, perhaps a duet of*
movement.

ORPHEUS
a bird draws a thread of sky
divides a lump of heart
infinitely

PROMETHEUS
and we sink upwards
but I knew your grasp

ORPHEUS
the god slackens the tightrope
and I walk
toward the other bank
with infinite caution

PROMETHEUS
listen to me behind silence

ORPHEUS
listen to me over silence

HEPHAESTUS
a rod rhymes with a rod

EROS
a piston with a piston

PANTHEA
a bolt with a thousand bolts

PROMETHEUS
but none of one sort with those of any other

HEPHAESTUS
(dialogue with the spectators)
This is the end of our rope.
Not we, but you will draw us out. Pull!

EROS
There must be something beyond the tunnel.

PANTHEA
Perhaps it is just what you expect.

HEPHAESTUS *has brought the end of a long rope out of the Tunnel and into the audience. As he and the spectators pull the rope, it pulls a hexagonal screen to the opening of the Tunnel. On this screen is now rear-projected the Myth Film, a silent film of images of the cast in the ruins of Rome which surreally illustrate* ORPHEUS's *spoken Myth Chorus.*

ORPHEUS
At four o'clock in the afternoon
1 pulled the past out of a well
I sang to it of the charms of love and labor
I conjured the daughters of Earth begotten by gods
the epic of the marble hand at the beginning of time
the ticking of Cronus
Niobe and her tears
the thousand skins of Proteus
clay bloomed into faces
I examined the habits of each face
looking for a clue
submerged in darkness
I lost friends hopes taboos
everything down the drain
everything beautiful everything perfect
everything dead

FURIES
(dressed as a reporter)
Was it the myth we expected?

PANTHEA
    It was the end of the rope.

EROS
    But try again.

PANTHEA
    (*hopefully*)
    There was, you know, some kind of promise.

FURIES
    Was there something we can remember without a shudder?

HEPHAESTUS
    Tug at your memory this time, at something,
    someone we can remember …

Spoken as in a dream, as if it were a phantom conversation. GANDHI
scarcely visible. HANON's *voice or* GANDHI's *echoing over tape?*
Then EROS *comes in and it gets realer-ish.*

FURIES
    Will not your movement lead to violence, Mahatma?

PROMETHEUS
    It may, though I am trying my best to prevent any outbreak
    of violence.

FURIES
    Don't you think your arrest likely?

PROMETHEUS
    It must be taken for granted. My arrest is a certainty.

FURIES
    A certainty?

PROMETHEUS
    When civil disobedience is started my arrest is a certainty.

FURIES
    You said some time ago that the time was not ripe for civil
    disobedience. What has happened between that time and

today that has helped you to alter your view?

PROMETHEUS

I am quite positive that it is fully ripe. The reason I will tell you. Nothing has happened externally, but the internal conflict in me which was the only barrier has ceased.

PANTHEA

But for women, Bapu, when will the conflict cease?

PROMETHEUS

My own opinion is that, just as fundamentally man and woman are one, their problem ... the fundamental conflict ... must be one in essence. The two live the same life, have the same feelings ... the one cannot live without the other's help...

EROS

Why then do you demand celibacy of the Satyagraha?

PROMETHEUS

In order to reserve that intense energy of love for the needs of our action—

EROS

When you confine me—

PROMETHEUS

Confine?—but it is only a temporary setting aside—

PANTHEA

To the prisoner is the reality of confinement ever temporary?

PROMETHEUS

I am a prisoner/ and I live in the future/ and ... and it is only temporary—

ORPHEUS

What do you see there?

PROMETHEUS

I see all of you—

The "Encounters" of Prometheus

Fire Music suddenly coming up; pause.

PROMETHEUS *rises and begins to descend on the Tunnel side, stage left; he is looking at the Tunnel; he begins to trance on the sound; the sound continues.*

PROMETHEUS
I see all of you.

Sound suddenly off; he pauses on the ladder, perplexed, but he is still trancing; he drops from the ladder and begins to cross the stage toward the Orpheum; the others gather round, coming from the theatre and Orpheum, looking up at him; FURIES *exits through house.*

PROMETHEUS
Through the lens of nature, moving the universe into place, I see you.

He stumbles and falls to the ground, convulsing, looking out toward the spectators; he begins to roll, slightly epileptic. PANTHEA *is coming on stage from the theatre.* PROMETHEUS *is trying to control his body. All look at* PROMETHEUS *and approach.* HEPHAESTUS *puts his palm over his eyes.* PROMETHEUS *is staring wide-eyed. They roll around together.* PROMETHEUS *rises and they move on the stage together.*

PROMETHEUS
Ahhhhhhhhhhhh
(*convulsing and moving with* HEPHAESTUS, *who has his hands over* PROMETHEUS's *eyes*)
I see the cords of disaster—
The untied knots—
I see the road to Paradise!
Ahhhhh—and so much blood—

HEPHAESTUS *pulls his hands away and* PROMETHEUS *breaks away from him;* ORPHEUS *seizes* PROMETHEUS *and puts his hand over* PROMETHEUS's *eyes.*

ORPHEUS
What do you see?

PROMETHEUS *turns toward him and looks at him intently even though* ORPHEUS'S *hand is ouer his eyes. Sound of music out.* PROMETHEUS *talks quietly now, leaning back in the arms of* ORPHEUS *and* HEPHAESTUS; *all move backwards, haltingly, as if imagining the things of which he speaks, as if he had never seen them before. He rises likes a somnambulist medium and begins to walk up the ladder; the others continue their backward movement.*

PROMETHEUS
... wheel ... arch ... alphabet ... motor ... harmonic bodies ... making of wordless wisdom ... oxes—smelting of ... heat against ice age ... *(Fire sound up.)*

HEPHAESTUS
Flame in Phoenix Park—

PROMETHEUS
Thermic invention, generation of motion, forging ...
(He suddenly slips on the ladder and comes out of his trance.)
It's gone—wiped out—like a vision.

Fire Music grows louder; FIRE *enters;* EROS *and* PANTHEA *are in Maithuna;* HEPHAESTUS *with* PANDORA; ORPHEUS *in Orpheum;* ORPHEUS'S *voice is heard periodically, low, during the Fire Dance, on tape, saying words from the Flame Poem section of* The Breasts of Prometheus.

FIRE *and* PROMETHEUS *dance together the Fire Dance. They are both naked. At the conclusion of the dance, they retreat together to the Fire Bouton, a small platform beneath the lip of the stage, stage center.* FIRE *burns and* PROMETHEUS *lies with him.*

34

"Hoi Prota"

All except FIRE *and* PROMETHEUS *cross from the Tunnel and from the Orpheum to center front dressed in flowing white doctors' robes, caps, and bibs. They carry a surgical tray and instruments.* ZEUS *brings a brain on a small pedestal. It is lighted from within. After the brain is ritually dissected, the* DOCTORS *process in two groups stage left and right with the two lighted halves of the brain. The brain halves are placed stage right and stage left at the foot of the proscenium, where they glow throughout the act. The* DOCTORS *process into the house. Throughout, they chant the "Hoi Prota" Chorus.*

THE DOCTORS CHORUS
> Hoi prota men blepontes eblepon maten
> who men at first exactly seeing saw vainly
>
> klutones ouk ehkouon all oneiraton
> hearing (they) did not hear but of dreams
>
> alingkioi morphaisi ton makron bion
> like images during the long life
>
> ephiuron eikeh panta
> (they) confused inconsiderately everything
>
> penteh schehmaton onton stereion haper kaletai
> five figures being solid which are called
>
> kai mathematika ek men too kubou
> also mathematical, from the cube (he) says
>
> gegone hegeh hek de tehs puramidos
> arose the earth, and from the pyramid
>
> ta pur ek de tou oktaedron gegoneh
> the fire, and from the octahedron the air
>
> ek de tou eikosaefron to hudor ek de
> and from the icosahedron the water, and from
>
> tou dodekaedron tehu tou pantos sphairon
> the dodecahedron the of everything sphere

35

The Titans

ZEUS, HEPHAESTUS, FURIES, *and* PROMETHEUS *return to the stage area.*

ZEUS

There are five solid figures
which are called mathematical or cosmic figures:
From the pyramid arose fire

(He places the pyramid on PROMETHEUS's *head; crescendo sound made by* ZEUS *and* PROMETHEUS.*)*

From the octahedron arose the air

(He places the octahedron on HEPHAESTUS's *head; crescendo sound made by* HEPHAESTUS *and* ZEUS.*)*

From the cube arose the earth

(He places the cube on FURIES's *head; crescendo sound made by* ZEUS *and* FURIES.*)*

From the icosahedron arose water

He places the icosahedron on his own head; crescendo sound made by all four thrice; as crescendo sound reaches its peak the third time and after two beats, PANTHEA *speaks.*

PANTHEA

There are five and only five figures
in the universe,
and, of these, the dodecahedron
is the most complex.

The four GODS *and* TITANS *make repeated crescendo sounds, remove their robes and, naked, mount stilts and move around in a chaotic pattern;* IO, HERA, *and* PANDORA *withdraw to the side.*

ZEUS

Once there was a test
when gods and mortal men

The mathematical figures, from left: Apollo Broom, Tom Walker, Julian Beck, Hanon Reznikov

divided **up** an ox.

PROMETHEUS
Prometheus set out the portions
trying to deceive
the mind of Zeus.

FURIES
He put pieces of meat
and marbled inner parts
and fat

HEPHAESTUS
And hid them
in the stomach
of an ox.

ZEUS
But when Zeus
saw the trick,
he raged

PROMETHEUS
  And took the fatted portion
  in his hands
  and vowed

FURIES
  Never to give
  the power of fire
  to humankind

HEPHAESTUS
  Because
  Prometheus
  loved them.

ZEUS
  And Zeus
  drove the Titans
  out of Heaven,
  (The TITANS *throw the stilts, eh eh eh ehh sound.)*
  Hurled wounding missiles

ALL FOUR
  and their shouting
  reached the starry sky.
  (crescendo sound)

ZEUS
  As there still remained one cosmic figure,
  the dodecahedron,
  God used it for the creation of the universe,
  broidering it with designs.

METIS'S VISION OF THE SKIES

Use of star sticks here, long wire poles with a tiny bulb at the end, powered by batteries in the handle.

TAPE (VOICE OF METIS)
> those little dots of light
> those little dots of light
> *(with telescope)*
> I am looking

TAPE
> those little dots of light going around Jupiter
>
> ZEUS *and* FURIES *descend from Pyramid.*

METIS
> Jupiter

TAPE
> change position nightly
> therefore they must be moons

METIS
> must be moons

TAPE
> like our own which circle us
> from this we can deduce
> that the earth is like a moon of our sun star

METIS
> when we look at Jupiter
> (ZEUS *and* FURIES *begin to wrap* METIS *up in a large cloth.*)
> we see a whirling turbulent mass
> of clouds and gases
> the sun's eye is a burning glass

METIS *gives the burning glass to the women—*IO, HERA, *and* PANTHEA.

WOMEN

(spoken in echo)

though they had eyes to see

METIS

(walk back)

they saw to no avail

WOMEN

(point and sway forward)

they had ears

METIS

(walk back)

but understood not

WOMEN

(point)

but like to shapes in dreams

METIS

(walk back)

to shapes in dreams

WOMEN

they wrought

(METIS *repeats.*)

all things

(METIS *repeats.*)

in confusion

(METIS *repeats.*)

(Aeschylus 442–445)

All walk backwards after each line.

The Jupiter Film begins, rear-projected on the screen in the front of the Tunnel; the film shows the red swirling light of Jupiter; the stage is dark except for the star sticks.

METIS

because Jupiter rotates faster at the

40

equator than at the poles ...
the spots are stretched out
into a conspicuous brightly colored band
the great red spot of Jupiter
has been observed for the last
three centuries/ it is of unknown
composition and unknown origin

EVE
the tiny earth plunges from the whirling stars

PANDORA
a spinner is spinning the orbits of all the stars

IO
the image of space changes the light
from a narrow one
to one that opens out
into the infinite

The Fire Wheel

Fire *begins to move.*

Pandora
Everything is woven on one thread

Eve
and history bears us through the ages
to rebuild persistently the anthill of culture
that history crushes underfoot

Film ends; the Fire Wheel is moved into place; the screen disappears into the Tunnel; the Fire Wheel is the front section of the Tunnel, about 18 inches deep, which comes away from the Tunnel and is now rolled on its six sides stage center by Hephaestus *and* Eros. Fire *is spreadeagled inside the Wheel, turned upside down as it turns.*

Pandora
and is no longer called stars
and creation and universe,
but sensations and imaginings,
or even experiences,
and conditions of the soul.

Io
It is shaped by a principle
whose name we do not yet know
of which we know only
an image shaped by the senses
the creative light

Prometheus
The sun's eye is a burning glass
(All the women *come to look.)*
does in the heart of tinder place
a real image of the sun
a mighty seed of fire
is entombed there

The Fire Wheel: center, Carlo Altomare; behind him, Ilion Troya;
Carol Westernik on Tom Walker's shoulders, Toby Marshall top center,
Rain House on Christian Vollmer's shoulders

    when smoke begins to pour and vomit
    look, with a puff, as if blowing itself alive
    flames are crazy with freedom
    which is the prize of wisdom

The WOMEN *light two small candles; as soon as fire burns,* EVE *goes
to get the taper.*

PANDORA
    this is the original light
    this is the light shown to Eve and Adam

IO
    All those deep and hidden things
    are not revealed
    till the word reveals them
    this word is speech and this speech is called Shabbos

(Io *sings the blessing in Hebrew.*)
up to this point
the male principle was represented by the light
and the female by the darkness,
but NOW ... they are joined together
and made ONE!

PROMETHEA

Thunder and lightning; ZEUS *rises; Fire Wheel is placed flat on the ground in the center.* HEPHAESTUS *crosses in thunder and lightning back to Orpheum.* PROMETHEA *entrance:* LILITH *storm; wind (fan); vibrating sound, veils flying, crooning sound; sung like a great aria; deep contralto tones or mezzo tones with moaning/crooning, in trance, like Mahalia Jackson; opera, but also a full trance; tragic.* PROMETHEA *enters from the Tunnel on the backs of* FURIES *and* EROS *as on a chariot; she circles the Fire Wheel; all sink down; she throws scarves to the* WOMEN; *she rides in pomp; ringing of bells.*

LILITH

    call me Promethea
    the beginning and the extinction of the world
    are not in me
    but they are also not outside of me
    they cannot be said to be at all
    since they are a continuing happening
    connected with me
    and directed by me
    my decision, my work, my services
    only she who believes in the world
    is given power to enter into dealings with it
    and she gives herself to this
    she cannot remain godless

Music of Zeus Enthronement; LILITH/PROMETHEA/HERA *ascends Pyramid; wind dies down; vibrating ends;* FURIES *slinks under Palace to his home;* EROS *and* HEPHAESTUS *return to Orpheum to make music and light.*

PANDORA

    What did they give you?

IO

    A flame of fire

and a tablet of
crystal

PANTHEA

What did you do with them?

IO

I buried them in a furrow.

PANDORA

What did you do with the flame of fire
and the tablet of crystal
after you buried them?

IO

I said words over them
(ZEUS *sees* IO.)
I dug them up,
I extinguished the fire,
I broke the tablet
I created a pool of water
(ZEUS *descends.*)

PANDORA

a pool of water

PANTHEA

a pool of water

ZEUS

I ask not about the meaning of the encoded message but
rather the meaning of the code chosen.

METIS

Just as an underwater swimmer has a very peculiar view
of the world above the surface, so for us contemplating the
universe, the image is greatly distorted

METIS *and* ZEUS *with telescope; blackout.*

ORPHEUS

A glass of water illuminates the world.

(Blackout; lights on; IO *runs;* ORPHEUS *takes arrow and in one move gives it to* EROS.*)*
Three times
A glass of water illuminates the world.
(Lights on.)

METIS
Light travels at about 360,000 kilometers a second.

There are three blackouts and lights on; IO *running and caught in the light each time;* EROS *delivers the arrow;* ZEUS *triumphs, points to* IO *vulgarly (sex/fire), and exits.*

The Ritual of Oriental Theatre

HERA *descends from Pyramid, sees* IO, *gestures. Walking toward the Orpheum, the arrow in her hand,* HERA *gives it back to* EROS *while speaking to* ORPHEUS.

HERA

Orpheus, there's a story of a woman transformed into a cow. I want to hear it now!

A batten is lowered upon which are draped the costumes and masks for the ritual. HERA *dresses as the Witch;* IO *as the nun, Chiyono;* ZEUS *as Kung, later transformed into Hermes, then Oceanus.* ORPHEUS *moves across the stage behind a constructivist screen through which only his head and arms appear.*

ORPHEUS

The scene is a bank of a river
The water is never the same
What we are at ten in the morning
We are not at noon
A philosopher king under a banyan
A priestess in a pasture
An empress in a pavilion
A moon in a sky

IO

The nun Chiyono
studied many years
but was unable to find enlightenment.

One night,
she was carrying
an old pail filled with water.

As she was walking along,
she was watching the full moon
reflected in the pail of water.

Suddenly

the bamboo strips
that held the pail together
broke,
and the pail fell apart.

The water rushed out;
the image of the moon disappeared
and Chiyono was enlightened.

She wrote this verse:

> This way and that way
> I tried to keep the pail together,
> hoping the weak bamboo
> would never break.

> Suddenly the bottom fell out.
> No more water;
> no more moon in the water—
> emptiness in my hand.

ZEUS
Kung walked
by the dynastic temple,
and then out by the lower river,
and Kung wrote on the bo leaves:
> If a man have not order within him,
> He cannot spread order about him;
> And if a man have not order within him,
> His family will not act with due order;
> And if the prince have not order within him,
> He cannot put order in his dominions.

PROMETHEUS
We elect administrators ... wise public servants,
experts, impartial ... who understand ... therefore
we must of course do what they advise ... but history has
perforce come to be ... out of control.

ZEUS *lifts the skirt of* Io.

HERA

(a pale scream)

That woman is weak or degraded is, I think, clear.

The passions of men have thus placed women on thrones, and till mankind becomes more reasonable, it is to be feared that women will avail themselves of the power which they attain with the least exertion ...

Besides, how can women be just or generous—how can I?—when they are the slaves of injustice?

(She screams again; she begins an incantation.)

I call on the help of the magician, Hermes, the trickster, the winged one,

Aid me in my plight

Apply your charms,

Your quick-changing metals, chemicals, metamorphoses.

ZEUS *is transformed into* HERMES; *he begins to walk in a magic circle around* IO; HERA *continues with her incantation of magic words.*

IO

Ah ... ah ... they are throbbing! My temples! Brain, migraine!

My ho head halls!

(Finnegans Wake)

HERMES

(holding the horned crown over her head; kenkehkeh sound.)

a stone lies in the road

tomorrow it may fly

the river changes and the sky

and sometimes the sky is a river

IO

Ugh, my feet, how heavy they've become!

My head's broken like a pail!

It's all illusion!

There is no moon in the water!

My brains have run out!

All feeling is folly!

The Ritual of Oriental Theatre: Mary Mary as Hera, Judith Malina as Io, Julian Beck as Hermes

HERMES
(crowning Io)
a woman becomes a cow
miracles walk among us;
a woman with horns on her brow
great fortune on earth and in heaven

Io
Your words don't move me.
I don't believe you.

HERMES *transforms into* OCEANUS.

OCEANUS
Me you can believe.
I am the sea.
Oceanus. The river god.
Your form is perfect.
Cowlike. And gentle.

What great destiny.
It is the mystery.
It is the truth.
And it floats through you.

HERA *approaches* IO, *wearing an old and wrinkled mask; she speaks gently.*

HERA

Ah, sister! Desolation is a delicate thing:
It walks not on the earth
It floats not in the air
But creeps with loving footsteps
It fans with silent wing
The tender hopes which in their hearts the gentlest bear,
Who dream visions of aerial joy, and call the monster, Love,
And wake, and find the shadow, Pain, as he whom now we greet.

Both women scream.

IO

This is not my true form!
I am not a beast! I am not an animal!
I challenge the order of this ritual!

HERA

Now wake.
Now you must go away from here.
I have no choice.
(Hovers over IO *like a fly.)*
I am driving you out of this country.
Out of the sight of my husband.
*(*ZEUS *turns.)*
I must protect...my hearth.

FURIES

Bzzzzzzzzzz

HERA *and* ZEUS *ascend to their thrones buzzing like flies;* FURIES *buzzes after* IO.

IO

    Ow! Ow!

    This is not an illusion!

ORPHEUS *dissolves the scene; the oriental costumes come off and disappear;* FURIES *and* IO *scream/buzz during* ORPHEUS's *poem.*

ORPHEUS

        Meditate on the changing lotus

        the lotus is the river

        an elephant is a handkerchief

        a woman is a beast

        and nothing is illusion

Io Pursued by the Furies
(The "Io Runs" Scene)

For Promtheus: *a trip in which he 1) expresses suffering, 2) examines it philosophically, 3) comes to understand the meaning of knowledge [God, or knowledge of God] through suffering; 4) transformed by this "marvel," he rebels: how can we/they end it? Question: Is he torturing* Io? *No. They are both taking the same trip in different forms. For* Io: *1) expresses suffering, 2) examines it philosophically, 3) transcends it: finds God; God-Creation; though she is greatly tortured physically, she tries to escape [against a pane of glass], but can't and then says:*

Io

> To say that suffering does good is false;
> *(Special emphasis.)*
> to say that punishment does good is false.
> *(She speaks up to* Prometheus.*)*
> Neither punishment nor suffering has any reality.

Io *goes to the proscenium; she drops her Chiyono costume; she is trying to get rid of fly; fly bites; tries to fight them off;* Furies *follow.*

Furies
> Bzzzzzzz

Io: *sound of pain—building to a first collapse.*

Prometheus, *on his rock, in pain position:* Prometheus, *bound, cries out:*

Prometheus

> The question is then, why do such things exist?
> *(turns away in inner reflection)*
> ... rather than nothing?
> *(change of voice: emphatic outcry of rage)*

Furies
> Bzzzzzz

Io: *Sound of pain;* Io *flees in a biomechanical movement; sometimes the scene is played onstage, sometimes it enters into the house and is played in the aisles.*

PROMETHEUS
(to self, with double awareness of his pain and Io*'s; dramatic moment on the Rock)*
The question is, how is everything a manifestation of the infinite love of God?

Io
It has driven all thought from my mind.

Philosophical recourse, calm tones; she looks at him; sound of pain.

METIS *and* PANTHEA *begin to move with* Io *in pain responses.*

FURIES
Bzzzzzzz

Io: *Sound of pain;* Io *falls against proscenium wall; not angry, but weak, wiped out.*

PROMETHEUS
(reflective, upside down, to self)
The question is, is the soul subject to pain?

Io
(incredulous, to self)
The question is, is this the order of the world? Is the world the order of God?

FURIES
Bzzzzzzz

FURIES*'s sound has been building lightly under* Io*'s last line;* FURIES *chases* Io *in a figure-eight out from and back to proscenium wall.*

PROMETHEUS
The question is, if everything has value, what is the value of suffering?

Io

    (*to* FURIES)
    The beings whom I love are creatures!
    (sound of pain)

HERA *joins in pain movement.*

FURIES

    Bzzzzzzz
    (He almost sweetens for a moment.)

IO: *Sound of pain; loud, first loud one;* PROMETHEUS *becomes aware of her.*

PROMETHEUS

    The question is, what crime if any are we being punished
    for when we are being punished?

FURIES

    Bzzzzzz

IO: *Sound of pain; the bzz and pain sound are brief;* IO *and* FURIES
now in Hot Spot, down center.

PROMETHEUS

    The question is, are you in contact with the supernatural
    or the natural?

Io

    I am suffering!

Sound of pain; FIRE *joins pain movement.*

FURIES

    Bzzzzz

IO: *Sound of pain.*

PROMETHEUS

    The question is, if the soul cannot be hurt, can it exist?
    My soul is a passage.
    (not challenging)
    Passage for what?

Passage for contact.
Contact with what?

IO

With whatever is God, with creation.
(sound of pain)

FURIES

Bzzzzzzz
(repeat)

IO: *Sound of pain;* HEPHAESTUS *and* ZEUS *join pain movement;*
FURIES *picks up* IO *in his arms.*

FURIES

The mind comes slap up against physical suffering,
(Bzz and gesture from IO*)*
affliction, like a fly against a pane of glass,
(Bzz and gesture)
without being able to make the slightest progress or
discover anything new, and yet unable to prevent itself
from returning to the attack. It is in this way that the
faculty of intuition is exercised and developed. Aeschylus:
"Knowledge through suffering."

PROMETHEUS: *revelation; he is transformed; is this the way to God?*

FURIES

Bzzzzzz

IO

(sound of pain; to FURIES *authoritatively)*
Put me down.
(to PROMETHEUS, *super-rational, beating him at the male game)*
To turn suffering into a sacrifice is a consolation ... but it is
then a veil thrown over reality. The same for punishment.
(slow Bzzz under this)
Neither punishment nor suffering have any significance.

IO *is saying to* PROMETHEUS: *punishment and suffering have no significance because the soul cannot be hurt [being immaterial, it is the instrument of transcendence], but* Io *is aware that reality is quotidian life, and she wants not only the soul, but also her human and woman's life to be free of suffering.*

FURIES

Bzzzzz

Io

(sound of pain)
I love reality. I want to go home.
*(*Io *runs; she stops—enough of this.)*

PROMETHEUS

How can we end human suffering?...

Io *begins to move.*

How Can We End Human Suffering?
(Tableaux Scene)

PROMETHEUS

How can we end **human suffering**?
(ORPHEUS begins Hell Cantata drum rhythm; PROMETHEUS remains on promontory and cries out.)
how
can we end
human suffering?
how
can we end
human suffering?

ORPHEUS

With the **invention** of the written word
the human **mind**
gave **birth** to all the arts

On ORPHEUS's lines the Oracle of Delphi Tableau forms.

PROMETHEUS

(from above)
how
can we end
human suffering?

Io

(as oracle*)*
suffering cannot be turned into energy
suffering can be turned into hate
and then
hate
into energy!

PANTHEA

the burning thought
enflames the mind

to act!

Tableau dissolves on PANTHEA's *lines; Hell Cantata movement to next position which is the Tableau of the Creation of Pandora.*

HEPHAESTUS
    The working hand
    draws out the light
    secreted in the earth
    The earth yields form
    and the form yields
    feelings and Fire

PANDORA
    When the clay comes to life
    the silence becomes dancing

FIRE
    If I have anything you want, take me: I'm free.

NARCISSUS
    Look for the angelic force in your face, in your eyes.

ZEUS
    Even God has his hell
    it is his love for man

IO
    I don't believe you
    your words don't move me

ZEUS
    Man was an experiment.
    Alas, how much ignorance and error have become human
    body in us

ORPHEUS
    The human mind at first stumbling and incoherent learned
    reason and consequence in the Promethean leap

Tableau dissolves.

EROS
    we're dying of the cold
    who locked me up
    in the Arctic?

As the actoresses move to next position, they stone EROS *to death;
as each actoress throws a stone, he/she stops whispering [the Hell
Cantata lines]; the Tableau of Crowd Looking at Accident Victim
forms.*

HEPHAESTUS
    when insufficiently supplied with oxygen
    the nervous system
    and especially the cells
    of the higher divisions
    of the central nervous system
    cease functioning; breathe!

NARCISSUS
    look,
    look at your face
    (He lowers mirror and looks at the dead EROS.*)*
    we all look alike

PROMETHEUS
    shall Zeus one day
    be hurled
    from his dominion?

Tableau dissolves.

METIS
    the burning thought
    enflames the mind
    to act

The Prometheus Bound Tableau forms.

ZEUS
    I want to teach you the meaning

the lightning of existence
it is the superman

Tableau dissolves and the Architrave Tableau forms.

PROMETHEUS
what land is this?
what people?
what crime
have they committed
that for penalty
they are doomed to destruction?

NARCISSUS
look! at your face
(flashing mirror up to PROMETHEUS*)*
look in your eyes
why do you avert them?
it contains the answer

NARCISSUS *moves toward the audience; Tableau dissolves.*

NARCISSUS SCENE

As NARCISSUS *speaks, he goes from audience member to audience member, showing them their reflections in the mirror; the other performers on stage move in a prearranged pattern to four different positions during* NARCISSUS's *lines; in the four positions they are equally spaced about the stage, standing in couples; each performer extends his/her arm and looks into the palm as if looking into a mirror; then after a beat, the performers look intently into each others' faces.*

NARCISSUS
I contemplate
I contemplate
where does the suffering come from?
I contemplate the universe
the horizon is in my eyes
I contemplate the ocean depths
where does the suffering come from?
look in your eyes
they are prayers
(moves from person to person.)
look at your reflection
make love to yourself
I am you

(position # 1; hold/look)
I am so moved by the beauty
that I want to unite
in a kiss

look, but not just a glance

(position #2)
gaze,
until the angelic force streams out of your eyes

(hold/look)

look, look at your face
now create your own character
look in the mirror of the water
try to grasp your own beauty
bend over the river of time

(position #3)
you can see all the forms
passing and fleeing

(hold/look)
now dream
look:

(position #4)
everything there is order and beauty
luxury, calm, and sensuality
do you want to see

(hold/look)
paradise?
look ...

FURIES
what you see is your ego
the defiance of God
you will sink
to the bottom
of mirror lake
and drown

FURIES *leaps into the audience and drags* NARCISSUS *down with him to the floor.*

HERA
don't believe them
they wrought all things
in confusion

PROMETHEUS
  what end is served
  by all the expenditure of suns and planets
  and moons, of stars and milky ways,
  if at last a joyous man
  does not involuntarily rejoice
  in his existence?
  (Goethe)

PANTHEA
  speak
  to me
  of woman

ZEUS
  (coming forward to PANDORA *with a gleaming box)*
  let the moons and the stars evolve in your love
  let your hope be:
  May I bear the Superman!

The Box Plays

PANDORA

this box is the world
(She steps forward and sits; she speaks intimately.)
It contains everything you know

ZEUS

We want to speak to you intimately

PANDORA

and everything you don't know

ZEUS

few occasions create the possibility

PANDORA

it contains the mystery
it contains the substance
(She takes out clay.)
from which I was molded
(She reveals the puppet, a naked woman figure.)
by Hephaestus
it contains Pandora

ZEUS

the possibility of communication

PANDORA

it contains the words of Hesiod:
(pointing with her right hand)
"From her comes the deadly female race."

ZEUS

the possibility of communication

PANDORA

it contains the forgotten and the yet to be known

ZEUS
  of communication between strangers

PANDORA
  it contains our visions; it contains the substance from which
  we are all made: energy ... and the 10,000 things of this
  world.

ORPHEUS
  it contains the mirror
  (He picks up his box and opens it.)

HERA
  we want to speak to you intimately

ORPHEUS
  the rocks

HERA
  few occasions create the possibility

ORPHEUS
  Hell ... the land of the dead, the past ... here.
  Here ... the live earth ... my world.
  (He switches on tape reader inside box.)

HERA
  the possibility of communication

ORPHEUS
  (taking out puppets)
  Orpheus—Eurydice

HERA
  of communication between strangers

ORPHEUS
  look in the mirror every day of your life and you will see
  death at work

HERA
  the theatre

ORPHEUS

Do you want to live forever?

That is the essence of poetry.

HERA

The theatre is such a place.

The box plays are played throughout the audience; the boxes are about 18 by 24 inches and 6 inches deep' most open at the back; performer takes objects out of the box and enacts with them a scene on the box in front of spectators as if on a little stage; the boxes hang at waist height around the performer's neck by means of a strap, in the manner of the nightclub cigarette vendor of many years ago.

ORPHEUS BOX PLAY

ORPHEUS's *scene begins during his Hell lines in the introductory chorus and continues simultaneously with the other box plays, which all begin immediately after the chorus.* **ORPHEUS**'s *"table" is half white, half black; it contains a small cassette recorder; it plays music; the table contains some musical instruments which* **ORPHEUS** *taps or plays at appropriate moments.*

ORPHEUS

the mirror

(He places an octagonal mirror which swivels at the center of the table.)

the rocks

(He places black rocks on one side and white rocks on the other.)

CHORUS

Few occasions create the possibility

ORPHEUS

Hell. The land of the dead. The past. Here.

CHORUS

of communication between strangers

ORPHEUS

Here ... the live earth. My world...

(He starts the music of the tape recorder.)

CHORUS
the possibility of communication

ORPHEUS
Orpheus
(He sets up an Orpheus puppet.)
Eurydice
(He sets up Euridice puppet.)

CHORUS
of communication between strangers

The tape recorder speaks: "Look in the mirror every day of your life and you will see death at work." ORPHEUS *holds the machine up to his ear and repeats the sentence.*

ORPHEUS
Look in the mirror every day of your life and you will see death at work

CHORUS
the theatre

ORPHEUS
(to audience)
Do you want to live forever?
That is the essence of poetry.

Chorus
The theatre is such a place

ORPHEUS *walks toward the audience and the intimacy scenes begin.*

ORPHEUS BOX PLAY, PART II

ORPHEUS
I sing! Because the celebration of beauty
is the answer to the invitation of death.
I sing to move the dead, to bring the rocks
themselves into life.

(sings)
Like the forehead of a star
(He opens the rocks as he sings; on them are written words; messages; the rocks speak.)
Love interpenetrates the granite mass ...
With the knife of her loneliness, Eurydice opened the mirror.
(Euridice puppet swivels into Hell; Orpheus puppet follows her.)
I entered Hell
I sang our way out.
(He sings two lines in Greek of a poem by Sappho.)
But the mirror flashed her with the look of eternity.
(Euridice puppet disappears again into Hell, which is hung around with black veiling; the black side of the box signifies Hell.)
And now
I sing and I will sing forever
Until light whose soul is fire
Melts the night in Hell.

PANDORA BOX PLAY
THE DEADLY FEMALE RACE

PANDORA
(She has begun her scene during the chorus.)
Not only did the Greeks consider Pandora herself evil, but she has a box.
(She places a small box in the hands of a puppet.)
Pandora opens the box and all the things of this world escape—all except hope. Now I'm going to open it again. I am going to let hope out. And we are going to hope, till hope creates from its own wreck the thing it contemplates.

Hope comes out of jail. Do you want to see it? Don't look for it in the air. Did you expect to see something flying around? Or a book on Utopia.
(She takes out a small book on Utopia, hand-made, and gives

*it out to spectators; she reaches into the box and her hand breaks
through the black paper which covers the hole on one side of the
box.)*
Here it comes.
*(Her hand sticks out on one side of the box and reaches toward the
spectators.)*
No, it's not my hand, the hope.
(The hand nears another hand.)
There it is ... It is that space between our fingers. It is the
invisible but undeniable force that compels us toward each
other ... It is free in this room. It is in your eyes.
(She touches someone.)
It is not in the touch itself but in the implication of the
touching. That we can not only touch each other without
intrusion, but that we can be at one with one another...
*(She touches and gazes at/with the people around her, going from
one to another; she forgets her box.)*
Why are your hands so cold? You need fire.

HEPHAESTUS BOX PLAY
DREAM MACHINES, WAR MACHINES

HEPHAESTUS

Hephaestus is compelled to make weapons. Just as we are
all compelled to support a military society.
(He takes out the Hephaestus puppet and many missiles.)
I don't want to do this. I have in me the hope not to be
doing this. I distribute these labels, in fact.
(He distributes anti-military labels among the public.)
I dream of making machines to realize our fantasies and
use fire power for machines that will not ecologically
jeopardize this planet and accelerate human suicide
(He reveals a bombed-out city.)
but will make use of solar energy without destroying life.
(He shows a solar energy machine.)

PANTHEA BOX PLAY
NOURISHMENT AND SLAUGHTER

PANTHEA's box has a plaque of lucite in the center, illuminated from below, on which she can paint. She begins to paint on it: a flowing sea/landscape.

PANTHEA

Limitless extension and oneness with the universe
oceanic feeling
 inseparable connection with the external world
(She sets little figurines of animals and birds out, also a piece of green cloth for the grass.)
it is the delicate spirit
that guides the earth through heaven
this is Panthea's vision
(She seats two female puppets in a corner, looking at each other, arms entwined; she lights a candle between the women.)
she sits here in this field ... with Asia, the fabled wife of Prometheus ... they are wrapped in love and they gaze at the sea and at each other and at the moon and are at one.
Fields of heaven-reflecting sea unstained with blood.
(She takes an eyedropper with red ink in it and begins to drop blood on the white animals.)
And the earth offers such a large supply of bloodless foods ... how can there be peace when we still find excuses to kill?
(She takes out two very thin, Giacometti-like figures of people.)
In order to raise this animal for the market required enough bloodless grain
(She takes out a scoop of grain and pours it on the table.)
to feed 200 people ... then the animal is killed.
(Blood drops on the animal.)
The people die for lack of grain, and the
sacred fire of life is drowned in blood.
(She smears red paint on the lucite.)

But in the box there is this hope
(She takes out a damp cloth or sponge, and wipes off the glass and begins to wipe the animals clean of blood.)
that our compassion for life will
wash over the errors and
(takes out a candle and lights it.)
rekindle
the vision which the red ink blots out.
(She blots out candle.)

Eros Box Play
Love's Dart

EROS

The force that through the green fuse drives the flower
(Dylan Thomas)
(He takes out a phallus, arrow-like, modeled after the sexual Tantric sculptures.)
It has a vector form. It crosses darkness.
(He rolls out a black felt band across the board indicating the Triassic Age.)
It crosses ice.
(He unrolls the Ice Age.)
It crosses jungles.
(He unrolls the Jurassic Age.)
It crosses the cement of our modern age.
(He unrolls the modern age.)
It is in search of union.
(He unifies with a Tantric yoni on the other side of the board.)
The whole story of evolution is at its base a love story. It appears in the dark as feeling.
Close your eyes.
(He closes his eyes and begins to stroke people around him.)
I appeared then—in the ice—as warmth.
(He takes the hand of a spectator and rubs it over his body from the

forehead down toward the genitals.)
It is said that I even gave people the idea in the first place
of making fire.
*(He takes out the stick and block of fire-making or a model of
people making fire and places them on the ice landscape.)*
because they associated making love with raising heat. Eros
stimulates the life force. That is my meaning. Eros is an
arrow that through the green fuse drives us on.

Io Box Play

*Io's table is bare, black, shiny; she takes out a ragged puppet; she
speaks.*

Io
A frightened woman moves wearily along the landscape.
*(She begins to distribute small black and white stones on the board,
tapping as she does so.)*
The landscape is beautiful like the moon.
It is bare and bone-strewn.
Every few steps she takes ... 1 ... 2 ... 3 ...
(At each step she taps a pebble.)
She gasps at the spectre.
(She takes out a ragged phantom, larger than her puppet.)
The spectre sometimes looms before her *(gasp)*.
Sometimes she sees it over her shoulder *(gasp)*.
Sometimes she sees its shadow before her *(gasp)*.
Sometimes the shadow crosses her and the woman sits in
the desolate landscape, overshadowed by the phantom,
which is real, and she worries.
(She seats the puppet.)
And she meditates on her condition.
And she hopes ...
And as she meditates, a dense mass of light accumulates in
her line of vision.

(She takes out a small intense blue-purple light bulb and places it before the puppet; she plucks some strings of a psalter-like instrument at the side of her table and sings.)
Light and heat,
who owns you?
Who's the master
of the dancing molecule?
The sun is in the sky,
the fire in the pyramid,
who will pay my bills?
(She takes out many bills from her drawer and shows them.)
The light bill and the gas … ?
(She makes a very high-pitched meditative sound.)

PROMETHEUS
What is that sound? Listen. Quiet, please, everyone.

There is quiet; she repeats the song.

NARCISSUS BOX PLAY
METAMORPHOSIS FLORAL

NARCISSUS *sets up a double-layer table, on the top a surface with a lake-hole in it; he sets up trees and grass and a romantic nature landscape; the puppet Narcissus should look like the actress playing the role. As he sets up the landscape, he speaks.*

NARCISSUS
These are the props of Narcissus. His world. Earth. Lake. Trees. Moss. Grass. Nature.
He is looking.
(He moves the puppet across the line of vision of the spectators around him.)
He is looking … into the lake.
He is in love, and that love generates a fire.
(He takes out a root lamp.)
Unbeknownst to him, large foot appears.

(He takes out a giant foot; the foot comes and tramples the Narcissus puppet into the lake.)
And he disappears one afternoon into the bottom of the lake …
no more consciousness.
(He blows out lamp and places it under lake.)
And Narcissus becomes a comedy. It is said that I metamorphose into a flower.
(He passes out Narcissus calling cards, flower cards; and he draws a flower out of the table.)
A flower that is trampled by careless feet.
(Foot tramples flower.)
But it cannot be forgotten that I was the force that through the green fuse drove the flower, that force, that fiery root, whose flame was drowned.

He holds out the extinguished lamp toward the public as if soliciting a light.

Hera Box Play

Hera sets a tape recorder going that makes a whirring sound inside her table; she places a large silver hoop in the center of her table; she pulls out a dark puppet—black chiffon—from a hole in her table; she whirls it into the air.

HERA

    She's an arc that starts
    in the primal dust.
    She's the mysterious exiled force of love
    visiting and returning
    (She whirls the puppet through the hoop.)
    comet-like;
    she, the primal female free-floating presence,
    Lilith, the first face.
    (She seats the puppet at one corner of her table.)

At the opposite end of the table
is the second face
of woman,
the great shining mother,
the apple-eating, serpent-listening, second-best rib lady,
Eve.
(She seats her opposite Lilith puppet.)
What can she do...
(She takes out a third identical puppet; she puts jewels on and peacocks around this puppet and seats it on a little throne in the third corner.)
... but accept the offer, sit on the throne, count her diamonds, and reign?
The third face: Hera.
Until the three unite ...
(She clutches all three together.)
... and pass through the transition range ...
(They go through the hoop; she ties them together)
... and reemerge ... as ... who? Who's coming out?
It's Promethea ... shhhhh ... the promethean in all of us.
(She sets herself on a silver slave ship.)
Who knows the signals for the takeoff?
She knows they are born only of a fiery energy which she seeks ...

She moves puppet along the eye-vision of the spectators.

Fire Box Play
The Question of the Use of Energy

Fire *lights a protected alcohol flame on his table in recessed cup; he takes out a black box and places it in the center of his table.*

Fire
    Fire, like love, is a release of energy, often slow in accumulating momentum ...

(He begins to move the box slowly.)

… and then suddenly coming to flame: a release, like love, of light and warmth.

(He removes the top of the box, the sides fall down to reveal a model of an atom.)

I am in there. I am in the atom. I radiate outwards.

(He unrolls a diagram of a brain—from Gray's Anatomy, the boutons of the brain.)

There is a fire in the mind. It exists here, in the cells of the brain. It leaps. It is a leap. It is a leaping. It flies. It is the Fire Bird.

(He takes out a Fire Bird puppet, radiant.)

It flies, this electrical bird, this fantasy of chemistry.

(He takes out several little birds on pins; some are flying, some are sitting.)

It flies from here, across here, to here.

(He places three pins on the bouton diagram.)

And from here to here, and from here to here and here … and that is the original fire.

And when it flies into the atom …

(He places a Fire Bird pin in the atom and takes out a picture of the fireball of an atomic explosion.)

… it releases a giant quantity of energy.

(He shows the picture, and crumples it and throws it away.)

It is a question of the use of energy.

PROMETHEUS BOX PLAY
THE ACCIDENTAL ADAM, THE ACCIDENTAL EVE

PROMETHEUS

Chance.

(He throws six yarrow or fennel stalks on his board.)

The pattern that these stalks make as they fall tells us the story of creation. The accidental.

What rich resources it contains. The pattern changes

(He throws the stalks again.)
and like chemicals being tossed again and again they
suddenly bring us—by swerve of shore and bend of bay—
to Eve and Adam's world.
(Eve and Adam puppets appear.)
And the creative force—what is it? Is it my hand right now?
The creative force tosses the elements again and again.
(He begins to draw a ragged smoky grey scarf out of the box.)
And a whirling mass of cold asphyxiating gas emerges, the
horseman of destruction; and Eve and Adam look again at
the faces of the world.
*(He moves the grey veil in front of the faces of the spectators, from
face to face, looking at the face, covering it, and looking again before
going on to the next face.)*
And Eve and Adam look for a way to preserve the ecstasy
of life, but it is getting colder,
and the tiny beings who stand halfway in size between
the atom and a star—terrified yet searching—strain to look
into the future.
*(He puts a crystal in the center of his board and circles Eve and
Adam around it.)*
And suddenly they become aware of a sound—a source of
noise.
What is that sound? Do you hear it? Shhhhh ... listen ...

ZEUS BOX PLAY
THE ORIGIN OF THE LAWS OF THERMODYNAMICS

ZEUS *takes out a puppet of a brain; it wears a long white gown; it is
suspended by a string; he sets up a landscape of metal and of skein;
the brain wanders about it.*

ZEUS
The brain wanders. It is searching. It is disembodied. It
observes. The center of seeing is here.

(indicates with a professorial pointer)
It speaks with a mouth, "Hello." It speaks with an interior mouth to itself. Agenbite of inwit. It speaks to itself in signs and symbols.
(He takes out a symbol of two double-headed arrows pointing at each other, joined in their center by a bar; he throws it on the table.)
Ananke: the two curved arrows: the struggle for existence. It confronts the night.
(black cardboard on small stick)
It confronts death.
(large black cardboard on stick)
And fear and misery come and tear at it.
(Either a steel fork or a torn glove tear at the figure.)
And it seeks to protect itself. It looks around. And it sees ...
(He looks over to where FIRE is.)
the Fire Bird and seizes it. And produces the passage of electricity from one generator to another.
(He switches on an electrical apparatus from which sparks fly out.)
And it has at last a feeling of safety.
(sigh)
And it protects the Fire Bird in a temple.
(He places the Fire Bird symbol on a small tripod between two columns.)
And writes the laws of thermodynamics.

He incants over magic Bird Temple.

FURIES BOX PLAY
SO MANY STONES

FURIES *takes out box after box, all of them sealed, grey, and black and metallic, filled with broken glass; the boxes are three-inch cubes; some are plastic; some have slime inside; some are covered with nails; some have dust inside;* FURIES *speaks with intensity and seething.*

Closed boxes. Sealed chambers. Forbidden sensations. Lost experiences. Closed doors.

(He picks up a box and reads off it.)

"It would be very nice, but how will we do away with sin?"

(He stacks the boxes.)

How does a child's mind get dusty? How can we clean the steps? How can we forget and how can we remember?

(He begins to look a little crazed; he begins to put the boxes on top of one another, pounding and slamming them down with a growing intensity and excitement—which sometimes subsides and grows again.)

Like the stones of the Great Wall
and the stones of the Pyramids
and the stones of Venice
and the barricades of Paris
and the Stone of Scone
and the stones of Stephen
and the stone of the great Kabala
and the stone around the neck of the kitten
and like the energy imprisoned in the stones
and the stones in the prisoners' field of broken stones!
All the cold, the flameless stones,
waiting for the fire of transformation to release the energy
and make them live.

FIRE THEFT

IO
(trailing out)
The light bill and the gas

FURIES
(dark, menacing)
Never to give the power of fire to humankind
Never to give the power of fire to humankind
Never to give the power of fire to humankind

CHORUS
Uh ... uh ... uh ... uh ... uh ... uh
(Continuing)

Voice of IO *trailing out: "The light bill and the gas."* FURIES *is heard: "Never to give the power of fire to humankind." Three times.* FIRE *ignites phosphorus or magnesium:* FLASH; *everyone slowly but intensely looks in his direction; they make a sound—"Uh"; slowly they all look at* IO; *"Uh"; then at* PROMETHEUS: *"Uh"; then at* ZEUS; *then back to* FIRE; *"Uh"; then to* PROMETHEUS—*"Uh"—* FIRE—*"Uh"—*ZEUS—*"Uh";* ZEUS *begins to move toward the stairs to the stage; he begins to mount; when he stands on the stairs or apron he points to* FIRE; *he and* FIRE *look at each other intensely;* FIRE *now begins to move onto the stage; they move deliberately;* ZEUS *in varying positions of high power and of the deities; in this manner they move toward the rear of the stage, backwards toward the Winter Palace (Pyramid);* FIRE *moves low and glides between* ZEUS's *legs into the bottom section of the Palace; when they have reached the center of the stage, the* CHORUS *begins to move forward, leaning forward, one behind the other,* PROMETHEUS *reaching out for the fire; they reach the stage and form two groups on the left and the right, backs to the audience, facing the fire; occasionally as they move they reach out toward the fire. As the movement begins, as* ZEUS *and* FIRE *are at center stage—*

HERA
  like air

PANTHEA
  and water

PANDORA
  and earth

METIS
  the fire
  belongs to those who need it

The CHORUS *continues to move in;* ZEUS *mounts the Pyramid; from his level he lowers a censer to* FIRE; FIRE *lights a flame in it which* ZEUS *raises and places on a small altar tripod on his right; he lowers it again and again* FIRE *puts fire into it which* ZEUS *raises and places on a left-side tripod;* ZEUS *assumes constantly the positions of Caesar and the gods; he is installing himself in his own temple; when he lowers the censer for the second time the people have almost reached it and try to take it, but he quickly pulls it above their heads;* PROMETHEUS *reaches up and snatches away the fire; he holds the removable cup of the censer in his hand.*

PROMETHEUS
  Tell us, O Wise One,
  if a man took away something and did not return it,
  would that be stealing?

ZEUS
  That would be stealing.

PROMETHEUS
  O Wise One,
  if a thing be taken and yet left behind,
  is that stealing?

ZEUS
  That which is left behind is not stolen.

PROMETHEUS *places the fire cup on his table, turns to the people and public, as in a puppet play; takes the burning cotton pellet from the censer's cup in a pair of tweezers, lights another flame inside the metal-lined fennel stalk which forms part of his puppet show, then ostentatiously returns the burning cotton pellet to the censer; ZEUS raises the censer and lights the second altar fire or places the flame cup on the second tripod.*

CHORUS

Narthaykopleroton deh theromai puros pegehn klopaian.
He hid it in a fennel stalk.
(outcry)

PROMETHEUS *passes the fennel stalk from one puppet table to another, and each table lights up a small flame or clicks on a yellow, orange, or red light or lamp; as* ORPHEUS *sings, all move toward the Orpheum.*

ORPHEUS

He hid it in a fennel stalk
and the cities glow
*(*FURIES: *Growling sound; roaring from the audience where he has remained after the other actoresses have returned to the stage.)*
He hunted out the secret source
and the cities glow.
*(*FURIES: *growling sound)*

ZEUS

You build the cities incorrectly.
(deity positions)

ORPHEUS

To curve of shore, to bend of bay
Korinth in her youth
Naples with her hope, her bloom

ZEUS

You dirty everything

ORPHEUS

In New York glowing in the streets,
lanterns of Diogenes,

84

in Delphi and Thebes,
in Rome ...
(Prato ... Dublin ... Amiens ... the city of the performance)

ZEUS
You soil the universe with stupidity.

FURIES
Never to give the power of fire to humankind!

PROMETHEUS
(speaking over the wordless melody)
Often my mother, Themis, the Earth—who has one form
but many names—told me how the future was fated to
pass ...

FURIES
(suddenly throwing his box contents on the stage)
Cities
sink
howling in ruin.

People freeze in paranoia; all eyes on PROMETHEUS; *faint Hell
Cantata rhythm.*

ZEUS
Take him out of the city.

FURIES *and* HEPHAESTUS *take the body of* PROMETHEUS, *in a
position of being rock-bound, and carry him across the stage to the
stage left ladder to the Rock; as they move,* PROMETHEUS *continues
to speak.*

PROMETHEUS
How it was not by brute strength
and not through violence,
but by quick clicking mind
that those who are destined to prevail
should find it that way.

FURIES *leaves* PROMETHEUS *at the base of the ladder to be led up to the promontory by* HEPHAESTUS; *he moves into the Hot Spot; Hell Cantata rhythm returns.*

FURIES
    Cities sink
    howling
    in ruin

ZEUS
    To the end of the Earth,

FURIES
    where blood
    with gold
    is bought and sold.

FURIES *continues moving frenetically; meanwhile, since the moment that* FURIES *throws his box, the people begin to move together at the Orpheum and form a mask of fear, spilling into paranoia; they move across the stage now toward stage left, barely moving their feet, very close to each other, eyes and mouths wide with fear, making a fear sound; they will move this way into the Tunnel.*

ZEUS
    The Scythian pale, that lone and ghastly land

PROMETHEUS
    What I did rose out of love.
    People were confused and without purpose
    until I taught them to develop mind and reason.

People begin to enter Tunnel.

FURIES
    Fire is left for future burning.
    It will burst
    in bloodless flashes.
    (caw caw sound)

ZEUS
    And now, Hephaestus, nail this law-wrecker to a sky-

86

piercmg crag.

Wind sound; HEPHAESTUS *begins hammering on metal clamps.*

PROMETHEUS
Mathematics, key to all the sciences, I told them, and the art of writing. The words came and the letters spoke.
(bang bang/caw caw)

FURIES
Past ages crowd on us,
the future is dark
and the present is dread.
(Bang, bang, bang; FURIES *picks up cord/rope left on stage or in audience from Myth Film.)*
We are tied to the past
just as we are tied to
these seats.
What wisdom can unbind us?
(Bang, bang, bang; FURIES *begins to tie up a member of the public with the rope.)*
What can we do
with our luminous words,
with our mathematics and splendor?
*(*PROMETHEUS *cries out.* HEPHAESTUS *leaves Rock.)*
With all our knowledge
of the psyche and of harmony?
(Snow cue)
What are we going to do
with our capacity to decipher
the burning signs?

FURIES *retreats to the stage, holding the end of the cord which is bound to the member of the public.*

PROMETHEUS
I saved the human race from death.
(caw, caw)

FURIES
What are we going to do?
Are we going to storm
the Winter Palace?
(blue lights)

People appear in the Tunnel, covered with snow; snow falls.

ORPHEUS
Act II. October, 1917. A Mass Spectacle.
The Storming of the Winter Palace.

BLACKOUT/CURTAIN

INTERMISSION

ACT II

PROMETHEUS BOUND

THE HISTORY
THE TRAIN AND THE SHIP

The sound of a train station, a babble of voices, sound of train pulling out, repetitive sound of rotating wheels. KRUPSKAYA, LENIN, *others moving down audience right aisle. Baggage.*

KRUPSKAYA

The train pulled out of Zurich with some thirty of us Bolsheviks on board. It was already the 8th of April. So much time consumed getting passports and visas. Now the Germans had let us on board without asking a question. llyich spoke hardly to anyone, kept entirely to himself; his thoughts were in Russia.

LENIN

Finally, finally, finally, finally, what I was born for is going to happen, what we've been preparing and preparing, what I've prepared the entire Party for and without which our whole life would be merely preparatory and unfinished.

CONDUCTOR'S VOICE

Stuttgart ...

Babble of train voices, train starts again.

KRUPSKAYA

You're right, the German government is under the impression that revolution would be a terrible disaster for any country ... and is letting us pass because they think it will help spread this in Russia.

LENIN

(speaking to USEYEVICH, *a comrade on the train with him)*
Our immediate problem is organization, not in the ordinary sense, but in the sense of drawing large masses of the oppressed classes into the organization, and of embodying in this organization military, state, and national economic problems.

CONDUCTOR

Stockholm!

KRUPSKAYA

Stockholm! Look, there's a red flag hung up in the waiting room! There's going to be a meeting.
(sound of train moving on)
I remember little of Stockholm. All thoughts were in Russia.
(Sound of train changes into sled sound.)
We crossed into Finland in small Finnish sledges.

LENIN

We have to get through ... we have to get through ... we have to get through ...

THE SHIP

Sound of a ship starting. EMMA GOLDMAN *and* ALEXANDER
BERKMAN *begin to move down the audience left aisle.*

SHIP'S STEWARD
(in American)
All aboard!

EMMA GOLDMAN
Well, Sasha—after two years in jail, they've decided to
deport us back to Russia. Do you remember how it felt to be
in prison in the United States when the Revolution broke
out in Russia? Now they have put us on a ship along with
fifty-one other anarchists born outside the United States
and are sending us back to be exiled in the land where we
were born. Twenty-eight days in a floating prison. January
1920. Ice. Snow. The days pass in a sort of trance. Bound
for Russia. Almost everything else is blotted out Matushka
Rossiya …

ALEXANDER BERKMAN
Matushka Rossiya. Mother Russia— Mother Earth. We
come back to you. Exiles. Emma Goldman and Alexander
Berkman are coming back to you. I am wild with joy.

*Lights on in the right aisle, down in the left aisle. Sound of train
again, train people continue moving toward the stage.*

CONDUCTOR
Bela Ostrov!

ZINOVIEV (FURIES)
(to LENIN*)*
Are you still afraid they might not let us over the border?

LENIN
No, they will let us pass. But when we get to Petrograd,
the Provisional Government may arrest us.

USEYEVICH (FIRE)
Look at how many soldiers there are out there ...
Hold your breath, everyone, this is it.

Train sound begins.

KRUPSKAYA
Kerensky's Provisional Government did not dare to stop
the Bolsheviks.
We entered Russia.

Lights down in the right aisle, up in the left aisle. Sound of train fades, sound of ship rises.

BERKMAN
Look, Emma, there, through the porthole ... there she is
... Russia ...

EMMA
Soviet Russia ... It's like a dream ... Imagine, Sasha, a free
workers' state ... isn't that some kind of contradiction? A
free workers' state!? I feel as if I were walking in a dream
... wake me ...

FINLAND STATION

The party of Bolsheviks begins to cross onto the stage.

KRUPSKAYA

Soon we arrived at the Finland Station. They urged me to
say a few words of greeting to the women workers, but all
words had left me ... I could say nothing ...
(The curtain opens. There are red banners and loud band music.)
There was a crowd of many thousands! Representatives of
the Soviet workers and soldiers.
Deputies came to meet us. They brought Lenin a bouquet of
flowers. Those who have not lived rhrough the Revolution
cannot imagine its grand solemn beauty ...
(LENIN moves across stage and stands on box.)
Vladimir Ilyich stood on an armored car and called out to
the huge crowd.

LENIN

On the trip here, I thought they would take us straight from
the station to the Peter and Paul Prison, but it seems to be
a very different picture ... The Proletarian Revolution is
imminent. We don't need any government except a Soviet
of workers, soldiers, and peasants' deputies! Long live the
world-wide Socialist Revolution!

EMMA

On January 18th, 1920 we arrived at the Finland Station.
We were welcomed with open arms.
(She is led to a box where she stands.)
Soviet Russia! Holy ground! Magic people! You have come
to symbolize humanity's hope!
You alone are destined to redeem mankind! I have come
here to serve you!

The Interview

There is a quick burst of music. Blueout.

EMMA

Months later, full of questions, we met the great Lenin.

LENIN

Sorry to have kept you waiting so long. I read your pamphlets with immense interest. Tell me, do you think there's any chance of a social revolution in America in the near future?
(BERKMAN attempts to speak.)
If there is a chance of social revolution in America, why didn't you stay there?
(He laughs.)

BERKMAN

But we did not leave of our own volition. We were deported.

LENIN

Deported!
(laughs)
I don't speak English.
(laughs)
Hardly a word. You speak Russian? Then let us speak Russian. Now that you're here in Russia how do you expect to contribute?

BERKMAN

There is something I must ask you: Why are anarchists here in the Soviet Union being kept in prison?

LENIN

But that's not true. There are no anarchists in prison.
(EMMA and BERKMAN attempt to speak.)
We have criminals in prison, and followers of Makno ... they are counterrevolutionaries fighting against the soviets.

Julian Beck as Lenin

EMMA

In capitalist America anarchists are divided into two
categories in just the same way—philosophic and criminal.
But I am under the impression that here there are comrades
of ours who are in prison for their ideas.

LENIN

There are no philosophical anarchists of ideas in prison
here.

EMMA

If there are anarchists in prison I will find it difficult to
work with the government. You must know that we

are committed to free speech and absolute freedom of expression.

LENIN

Free speech! Free speech is a bourgeois luxury. I think you have a sentimental view of it.

(laughter)

In a revolutionary situation economic well-being speaks louder than speech. Textiles, nails, salt, machines, tractors, wheat, electrification: when we can give the people these things—then they will be on our side. But for the moment free speech in Russia is merely a tool for the reaction—a means of weakening Russia. And anybody who does that must be kept under lock and key ...

(laughter)

(EMMA crosses the apron and begins to walk up the stage right aisle. BERKMAN begins to climb to the Promontory.)

I urge you to take up some useful work and regain your revolutionary balance.

EMMA

(as she leaves, sound of train ...)

We left Russia in 1921. They put us on a train for Latvia.

BERKMAN

(climbing)

Days of anguish. My heart is numb. Something has died within me. The Bolshevik myth is dead. I am with those in prison and as long as there is anyone in prison, I am not free.

PROMETHEUS

(BERKMAN on Rock)

Do what he will, I am one he cannot kill.

(repeated in Greek)

EMMA

(halfway up aisle)

It was all an illusion ...

The Storming of the Winter Palace

Lenin/The Actor Playing Lenin
Lights, please.
(Lights up on stage.)
Lights in the auditorium also, please.
(Lights up in the theatre.)
What we want to do now is stage the Storming of the Winter Palace. That, of course, is not something that a few actors can do. It must be a mass spectacle. And above all, of course, it must be organized. We want to do this as a mass spectacle with your participation. Everyone will play his role.
(enter Fire)
This event occurred less than six months after Lenin's arrival at the Finland Station. It was THE DAY. The 25th of October. We want always to be historically accurate, and we want to include some of the events that led up to the seizing of the Winter Palace, and we also want to play some scenes representing events that were consequences of that event.

The majority of people will be needed to play the people themselves and the army in the action of the actual storming. The actions that you will be called upon to do will be emblematic, because we want to symbolize its style. Map, please.
(Map is lowered.)
This is an aerial view of Uritzky Square and the Winter Palace and a diagram of the general plan of "The Storming of the Winter Palace" when it was performed as a mass spectacle on the third anniversary of the actual storming. This mass spectacle was directed by Nikolai Evreinov with Petrov, Kugel, and Annenkov as assistant directors. The entire square was decorated with constructivist designs by

Nathan Altman. The spectacle involved 8,000 people as actors including army units, armored cars, army trucks, and, on the exact historical spot, on the Neva, the battleship *Aurora*.

It was here in the Winter Palace that the Provisional Government of Kerensky was making its last stand. I should add that the performance was said to be better organized than the actual storming of the Winter Palace, which was said to be full of confusion.

I would now like to explain the scenes, then we will separate into different groups to rehearse the scenes, and then we will put them together. First I should list the six special groups and describe their work in detail. So, in addition to the large mass, we need six groups of four to ten people each to play the Terrorists, the Bolsheviks, the Anarchists, a group of Tolstoyan Pacifists, a group of Russian Women, and a group of circus performers.

1) Four people to play the NARODNIKS, the terrorists who were active during the last three decades of the nineteenth century. Politically, they were socialistically inclined, of course, and had a libertarian coloring, but had no problem with the question of violence. The action includes some physical movement, and you should meet with ILION— FIRE—over here at the mouth of the Tunnel. Are there some people who would like to play that? Good. Could you come up here now?

2) Next, the BOLSHEVIKS. The work is mostly choral. There are some printed texts—with musical cues—no, you don't have to sing, but some good strong voices would be helpful. And you should meet over here on the left—on your right, rather—by the edge of the proscenium, to work with MARY—KRUPSKAYA—and TOM—ZINOVIEV. MARY will have to leave you occasionally when she plays the

CZARINA or KRUPSKAYA. KRUPSKAYA, of course, is LENIN's wife and comrade, co-worker. Much of the material for this act is taken from her memoirs of Lenin, as well as from the memoirs of Emma Goldman, and from several studies of the Bolshevik Revolution—chiefly works in English, E. H. Carr's classic history of Soviet Russia, Trotsky's records, and several reputable biographies of the protagonists. So can we have eight to ten people come up here to play the party members?

3) A group of ANARCHISTS. If you could meet in the balcony with HANON, their action is both physical and vocal. We don't want too many because we want to try to keep the proportions correct, and the Anarchists were not a majority group; we remember that the word *Bolshevik* means in fact majority in Russian. And so they shouldn't be too large a number. Are there six volunteers? No, there are too many—fabulous—so many people who want to play the ANARCHISTS! What a zap! When we divide to go into rehearsal would you—anarchistically—decide who is going to play the ANARCHISTS and who among you will come and join the people here in the theatre for rehearsal?

4) And now—the PACIFISTS. We want to represent a group of Tolstoyan pacifist anarchists. You will work with MARIAROSA ARNOSTI, with PANTHEA, with the imagination, and with universal love. I think that there is a space in the back of the theatre where you can work.

5) A group of women to play both the oppressed and imprisoned WOMEN. You should meet first on the stage here with IMKE—IMKE, who played METIS in the first act of the play and who is still back there in the prison. There will be a liberation scene and IMKE will organize that with you. I think about twenty women will be sufficient. Only three, I think, can fit in our palace prison, but the others

will have a special scene to play.

6) We need a small group of people, three to six only, I think, to play members of the Moscow State CIRCUS in a performance of Mayakovsky's play "1905—Moscow Is Burning." The play was originally performed in 1930, and the poet shot himself to death one week before the opening. He had been rehearsing the play intensely at the time. There are some acrobatics involved. If you could meet here at the Orpheum—with CARLO, who plays MAYAKOVSKY and the poet ESSENIN. Oh, by the way, we wanted to rehearse these scenes in fifteen minutes only, so we must discipline ourselves to use the time economically. Otherwise we may be here all night and we may never get to storm the Winter Palace, which would be a disaster.

If theoretical questions occur, send them to EMMA GOLDMAN.

I myself will try to organize the actual assault. I would like to divide the theatre itself in half—and on the right side all the people who want to play the poor and the workers who take part in the assault on the Winter Palace. At some times I will be playing LENIN, at some points TROTSKY, and at some points the CZAR.

Is everything clear? Good, then let's go to our places and return here—let's synchronize our watches; in exactly twenty minutes let us assume that everyone will be in place and that we will be ready to begin.

JULIAN *and the actors, including* PAUL/HEPHAESTUS, *organize four different groups for the assault on the Winter Palace. The four groups: the* ARMED WORKERS, *the* RED ARMY, *the* 2ND BATTALION, *and the* INFANTRY.

~ THE REHEARSALS ~

JULIAN

(after twenty minutes, checking that everyone is back and in place)
Good, we all seem to be here. Now, the technique that we
have planned for the playing of this is related to the montage
techniques developed by the great Russian cinéastes. We
will go rapidly from scene to scene, sometimes going
backwards and forwards in time. So please pay very close
attention to your cues: when your scene is called, begin;
when it is over, freeze and wait for your next cue. Things
will happen that you do not expect; they always do. But
this is part of it. If we're all ready then, let's go. Lights
please, music. The Storming of the Winter Palace.

Scene 1: March 1898, Minsk

ORPHEUS

October begins in February
1917 begins in 1905
1905, said Lenin, was the Great Rehearsal,
for which rehearsals began long before.

Scene Number 1:
March 1898: the city of Minsk:
the founding of the Russian Communist Party.

The BOLSHEVIKS, *a* CHORUS, *stand stage left, near the proscenium edge. The leader of the* CHORUS *is the* FURIES/ZINOVIEV. *The* CHORUS, *from the public, have scores for their sequences printed as small booklets to guide them.*

FURIES/ZINOVIEV

A party binds.
We are throwing out a rope.
(*He throws out a rope to* FIRE.)

BOLSHEVIKS

Nine men/ meeting in Minsk/ deciding to form/ not a group/ but a party.

KRUPSKAYA

The Russian Social Democratic Workers' Party.

ZINOVIEV

All were arrested
(*Their hands go up.*)
and never played much of a part again in the story of
the party and the revolution.
We had done enough.

They turn around and begin slowly to pull red scarves out of their breasts or clothing. The leader pulls at the rope.

FIRE

(*being pulled in*)

It was the spark ... which led to the foundation of a weekly newspaper called ... *Iskra*. The spark.

He throws out rope; it begins to pull in LENIN.

LENIN
We must solidify the Social Democratic Workers' movement.
We must take up the work abandoned in 1898
and summon a Congress and draw up a Party Program.

LENIN *throws out the rope again to the audience. Blackout/gunshot; lights on in Tunnel.*

Scene 2: Petrograd, March 1, 1881

ORPHEUS

How many bullets are there in it?
(machine gun fire)
I sing of arms and the man.
(He repeats the line in Latin.)
Arma virumque cano.
(Virgil)
A bullet asks only one question;
And how many answers has death?

Scene Two:
Petrograd. March 1st, 1881.
(LENIN crosses to the Pyramid.)
The Assassination of Czar Alexander II by the group which
called itself Narodnaya Volya, the People's Will.

This scene is played by the group of TERRORISTS, *rehearsed by*
FIRE. *They sit crouched in the Tunnel. They carry flat black masks
made of cardboard or see-through cloth stretched over a frame. They
carry wooden pistols made crudely, like children's hammered-together
toys. They emerge furtively to a beat-like repetitive sound, perhaps
electronic. They move from place to place on the stage at each beat.*
JULIAN/CZAR *and* MARY/CZARINA, *wearing the Order of the Star
of Russia, etc., the* CZARINA *a tiara, mount the Pyramid. Sound
cue: the* TERRORISTS *take a step.*

FIRE

I do what I do out of love!
(sound cue, movement.)
I throw myself toward the people.
(sound cue)
Tragedy as vehicle of enlightenment!
(sound cue)
The Great Liberator is coming!

The TERRORISTS *take aim, shoot, or throw imaginary bombs. The*

CZAR *falls from the Pyramid. The* CZARINA *screams.*

CZARINA
My God! They've blown off both his legs!

CZARINA *sinks, kneeling, crossing herself. The* TERRORISTS *move to the curtain line and stand straight across in front of it, holding up their masks.*

FIRE
The act was executed by Narodnaya Volya. It was

TERRORISTS
The People's Will.

FIRE
(to public)
The question is:
Can you do the wrong thing
for the right reason?

Scene 3: Moscow, 1892

ORPHEUS

To the bullet which has only one question
What is the answer?

Scene Three:
Moscow. 1892. The Anarcho-Syndicalists rehearsing
the Great Play.

The scene is rehearsed by HANON. *The* ANARCHISTS *begin to move
under people's feet all over the theatre.*

EROS

Is there something moving under your feet?

2ND ANARCHIST

Does the ground seem to be shifting?

3RD ANARCHIST

Don't look at the sky.

4TH ANARCHIST

Look down.

5TH ANARCHIST

Look at the earth.

6TH ANARCHIST

Something is rising …

EROS

It is the movement for an ownerless earth …

2ND ANARCHIST

Ownerless land …

3RD ANARCHIST

Ownerless people on it.

ALL TOGETHER

It is rising …

Lights slowly up in balcony. EROS *calls across the theatre to the* TERRORISTS.

EROS

To the comrades of Narodnaya Volya:
Small groups cannot perform what must be done by large masses.
Acts of terror embitter the workers and nourish coarse and bloodthirsty instincts!

PROMETHEUS

(on the Promontory, writing a letter in prison)
Dear comrades, I call out to you from the Peter and Paul Fortress. You must propagandize among the workers, among the peasants. Here in prison it becomes clear what the state is: it is not order but the lack of freedom. Tell them that!

EROS

The immediate mission of Anarchism is to organize revolutionary labor unions.

The ANARCHISTS *are in the aisles, moving toward the front of the theatre.*

JULIAN

(coming forward as stage director, pointing out a section of the audience)
Very good!
Let us assume that the people out there are a group of workers in a factory.
(now to the ANARCHISTS*)*
And that you're going out there to organize a revolutionary workers' union. What do you say to them?

The ANARCHISTS *distribute leaflets among the audience section, documentary texts from Paul Avrich.*

EROS

Autonomous society. Freedom to organize yourselves, freedom to decide how the work we do is done.

2ND ANARCHIST/HEPHAESTUS

Freedom not to work if you don't want to.

EROS

And always enough to eat even if you don't work.

PROMETHEUS

We are dealing with the most delicate of balances, the balance between the individual and the collective. The secret of life is freedom and the secret of freedom is courage.

JULIAN/LENIN

Do you believe them? What d'ya choose? Huh? Do you choose terror? Do you ... choose infantile idealism? Or do you choose a Workers' Party?

Scene 4: Odessa, 1895

ORPHEUS
Scene Four:
Everything is small
The party is small
The anarchists are few
The terrorists are fewer
And the peasants who are the most
are the smallest.

Odessa. 1895. A group of Tolstoyans
scything the wheat.

Lights down except in the Tunnel. The TOLSTOYANS *come through the Tunnel with scythes, moving biomechanically across the stage. They come to a stop at the curtain line in between the* TERRORISTS.

ORPHEUS
(singing)
The song of the wheat
(sound of scythe)
is the song of the body
(sound of scythe)
and the song of the body
(sound of scythe)
is the song of the mind
(sound of scythe)
and the song of the mind
(sound of scythe)
is the song of the heart
and the song of the heart
is the song of the spirit

PANTHEA
(She leans on her scythe, mops brow.)
There is a misery of the peasant and a misery of the factory
hand.

109

LENIN

(at lectern)

The star of the industrial worker is rising.

PANTHEA

Both work long hours and receive small pay.

LENIN

The star of the peasant is waning.

PANTHEA

But the factory hands are deprived of freedom, because they do not have contact with the nature which is free. I am quoting Tolstoy.

LENIN

Too many peasants do not realize the inevitability of the dictatorship of the proletariat.

PANTHEA

And the Marxists wish to industrialize the peasants.

LENIN

And it is the industrial proletariat which best expresses the real interests of those who toil under capitalism.

(Fischer, p. 379)

PANTHEA

Because regimented labor serves better a program based on violence and obedience.

FIRE

(replying)

But governments themselves are organized violence.

PANTHEA

Up to now, all attempts to get rid of violence have always resulted in new governments more cruel and more violent than the ones they replaced.

PANTHEA *looks at* FIRE *deeply and suddenly, impulsively kisses him on both cheeks. The other* TOLSTOYANS *do the same to the other*

110

TERRORISTS, *whom they recognize because they are carrying masks. They then proceed into the aisles and mow their way to the back of the theatre, and into the balcony.*

ORPHEUS
(singing as they mow their way up the aisle)
The song of the heart
(sound of scythe)
is the song of the spirit
(sound of scythe; ORPHEUS continues song.)

FIRE
(calling after them)
This gun is in my hand only to liberate you.

PANTHEA
Will it liberate you?

TOLSTOYANS
(repeat to audience)
Will it liberate you?

Scene 5: Petrograd

ORPHEUS

When the radio talks about terror do you pause to hear more?
Do you ask yourself why?
In the cafe at the corner do you think ...
if a bomb flies in through the door ... ?

Scene Five:
Petrograd. The arrest of Alexander Ulyanov,
Lenin's brother,
for a plot against the life of Czar Alexander III.

FIRE

With an amateur chemist's bomb I proposed to assassinate the Czar.

FIRE *turns and leaps, once, onto the stage toward the Pyramid, with bomb in his hand. As* FURIES *talks,* TERRORISTS *freeze and* FIRE *drops bomb in hands of confederate.* BOLSHEVIK CHORUS *claps after each phrase.*

FURIES

The plot was discovered. Arrest came on March 1st, 1887. The prisons were swollen with terrorists. At his trial, he said:

FIRE

(turning and facing the public)
The intelligentsia is so unorganized that it is only through terror that it can defend its right to intellectual participation in society ... It is the unavoidable consequence of existing contradictions of life ...

FURIES

He was hanged.

BOLSHEVIKS *clap.* FIRE *twists around quickly 360 degrees and assumes position of a hanged man.*

LENIN
(at lectern)
We have never renounced terror and cannot renounce it.

FURIES
Bombs exploded in cafes,
(clap)
restaurants,
(clap)
theatres ...
(clap)

The TERRORISTS *throw a mock bomb into the audience and then run into hiding around the theatre.*

FIRE
(running)
There are no innocent **bystanders!**

SCENE 6: FEBRUARY, 1917

ORPHEUS

It's getting closer
like a cloud ... or a train ...
or ... curtain time.
Title: The Second Storm:
February 1917:

Scene Six:

Led by LENIN, *the insurgent people who are in the seats of the
auditorium begin to chant, one side of the audience alternating with
the other:*

PEOPLE

Bread/ Strike/ Bread
Bread/ Strike/ Bread
Bread/ Strike/ Bread

Placards are distributed by members of the BOLSHEVIK CHORUS *and
by the* ANARCHISTS. *The texts for the placards come from Avrich,
Fischer, Valine.*

FURIES *assumes the role of* LENIN's *associate* ZINOVIEV; *the*
BOLSHEVIK CHORUS, *those not distributing placards, punctuate his
phrases with a sound.*

FURIES

From early morning/Whoomph!
Whole regiments of the Petrograd garrison/Whoomph!
Mutinied/Whoomph!
Seized the government arsenal/Whoomph!
And occupied all vital points in the city/Whoomph!
Czarism had fallen/Whoomph!
Czar Nicholas signed his abdication/Whoomph!
Was arrested/Whoomph!
And the royal family eventually executed(Whoomph!

(His voice changes in quality, clear.)
A Provisional Government led by Kerensky was proclaimed.

Sound: "La Marseillaise"; the ANARCHISTS *with black banners stand at the head of aisles, in balcony, waving the banners.*

EROS
> I come to you with greetings
> To tell you that the sun has risen!

FIRE
> *(waving anarchist banner)*
> The gods are dying!
> Long life to the people!

PROMETHEUS
> *(calling out from promontory prison)*
> Do you know the process—apart from sheer destruction—
> which will transform the old forms into new ones?
> (Alexander Herzen)

FIRE
> *(In balcony; as he speaks, black banners or placards are saying, "Down with Authority & Capital.")*
> We are setting up anarchist cells in three large munitions plants.

PROMETHEUS
> Who steers necessity?
> MOIRA. The Triple Fate, and the Furies,
> who never forget! Retribution!
> *(He groans in anguish.)*
> But Zeus himself matched against them is weak
> and will not rule forever. Is that true?
> No talk of that ...
> No further questions ...

Scene 7: July, 1917

ORPHEUS

Premonitions become laws,
flights, arrests, disguises.

Scene Seven: July 1917:
Lenin in a wig.

CHORUS LEADER (FURIES)

The Police again!

The CHORUS *scatters and hides around the theatre.*

KRUPSKAYA'S VOICE

Our place was searched for the third time while I was away.
Ilyich was in hiding
*(*LENIN *into the Tunnel where he sits, working.)*
at the house of an old member of the underground party
organization; the Bolshevik Party was reduced to semi-
illegality. These were the July days. He decided to cross
over to Finland. He wanted to work on his book, *State and
Revolution.*

EMMA GOLDMAN

(in the audience in a blue light)
Comrade Lenin, Comrade Lenin, on the eve of the
Bolshevik revolution, tell us, what do you foresee ... ?

LENIN

(in a blue light, writing)
I am writing that now ...

EMMA

In 1905 you wrote, and I quote, "We have need of
revolutionary power, and for a certain period of transition
we have need of the State. In this we differ from the
anarchists ..." Tell me Comrade, how long do you foresee
this transition period must last?

116

LENIN

"The proletarian state will begin to disappear immediately after its victory—since in a society without class contradictions, the State is unnecessary and impossible." That's from the pamphlet I'm working on now ...

EMMA

Do you know what I foresee? I'd like to read you a letter I wrote to Alexander Berkman ten years after the Russian Revolution. "My dearest Sasha ... when in the first days of our Russian life, still believing in the old form of revolution, I once said—I remember the wording very distinctly: 'If revolution cannot solve the need of violence and terror, then ... I am against revolution.' You flew at me with rage and said I'd never been a real revolutionist. Well, now you seem to have come to the same conclusion. But we are loath to let go of the thought of revolution in terms of destruction and terror. And that I am done with for all time. I insist if we can undergo changes in every other method of dealing with social issues, we will also learn to invent new methods of revolution itself. I think it can be done ... If not, I shall relinquish all my belief in revolution. Such a waste of human lives, such an endless repetition of the old refrain, 'The French Revolution Was That Way, All Revolution Must Be That Way.' "
(BOLSHEVIK CHORUS *begins sneaking back to its place.*)
History dictates our course. History has become the new superstition. Like the will of god. I no longer believe in that, dear Vladimir Ilyich ...
(EMMA *light down and out.*)

KRUPSKAYA'S VOICE

On October 7th Ilyich moved back to Petrograd.

The CHORUS *begins slowly to reach its original position, stage left.*

FURIES/ZINOVIEV
The Central Committee approved a resolution in favor of

CHORUS
Armed insurrection!

KRUPSKAYA
At 22:45 on October 24th, the eve of the Deciding Day,
Lenin, disguised as a worker, wearing a wig,
(LENIN *leaves the Tunnel.*)
arrived at the meeting of the Petrograd Soviet.

LENIN
(*disguised, arrives at the* CHORUS *position*)
Has the Fleet arrived in the Neva yet?

ZINOVIEV
Yes.

KRUPSKAYA
llyich, they want you to speak. You can remove the wig
now.

LENIN
Not yet. I will. When the Winter Palace falls.

SCENE 8: OCTOBER 25, 1917

ORPHEUS

Scene 8: October 25th 1917:
The Storming of the Winter Palace.

FURIES

(rapping with the gavel on lectern)
Comrades, a statement on the situation by Comrade
Trotsky.

JULIAN

(at lectern with TROTSKY *mask)*
I'm playing Trotsky now. This is from the speech he made
around one o'clock that day to the Petrograd Soviet:
"The government is still in session at the Winter Palace,
but it is no more than a shadow. On behalf of the Military
Revolutionary Committee, I declare that the Provisional
Government is no longer extant.
*(*BOLSHEVIK CHORUS *applauds.)*
Some ministers have been arrested.
*(*CHORUS *applauds.)*
The citizens slept in peace ignorant of the change from one
power to another. The Railroad Station, the Post Office,
and the State Bank have been occupied.
*(*FURIES *and* CHORUS *make loud applause.)*
The Winter Palace has not yet been taken, but its fate will
be decided during the next few minutes."
(as stage director, coming forward)
Now, the distribution of guns and ammunition to the
factory workers. The Revolutionary Military Committee
distributed ammunition to the workers in factories
sympathetic to the Bolshevik program.

FURIES *and* BOLSHEVIKS *attach red ribbons across the stage: from
proscenium left to proscenium right, from left tower to right tower,
from Tunnel to Orpheum, from Tunnel to Pyramid, etc.*

JULIAN

Lenin now convinced the Committee—still wearing his wig and disguised as a worker—that they could no longer be indifferent to the question of armed insurrection. With Trotsky he organized the revolutionary military committee which made military preparations for the revolution. We are drawing five tapes across the stage. As the Storming of the Winter Palace progresses, the tapes will successively be broken or cut. Everyone in their places? The Storming of the Winter Palace!

FURIES

1:25 pm. The first attack by the Red Guards or armed workers. Armed workers attack!
(The ARMED WORKERS from the audience rise and begin to move deliberately: 1-2, 1-2, 1-2, 1-2 ...)
Fire!
(sound of bullets)
Break the first tape!
(An ACTOR/AUDIENCE MEMBER cuts the first tape with scissors.)
The Junkers guarding the Palace return fire!
(sound of bullets)

EROS

(from above)
An unknown number fell. Not many by military standards. Some of you down there must lie down and play dead.

FURIES

(speaking rhythmically)
2:00 p.m. The army arrives. Would the RED ARMY take places?!
(AUDIENCE PARTICIPANTS take places.)
Trucks of soldiers are arriving, contingents of armored cars are arriving and soldiers are arriving through the Narva Gate. Begin the attack!
(A larger number of people, three times as many, come onto the

120

*stage; they make a battle charge sound; they cross the stage: 1-2-3,
1-2-3 … and cover it.)*
Fire!
(on tape, sound of machine gun fire, shelling, battle noise)
Break the second tape!
*(*AUDIENCE MEMBER *cuts second tape.)*

EROS
(sprinkling bits of red paper)
I'm spilling blood. Whoever gets touched by one of these
bits of red paper has been shot and must lie down as if dead.

CHORUS
The Winter Palace
Home of the last Czar
The seat of the Provisional Government
Still holding out …

KRUPSKAYA
… and it's almost midnight.

FURIES
The Palace was surrounded.
SECOND BATTALION on stage! SECOND BATTALION forward!
SECOND BATTALION on your bellies! SECOND BATTALION
Fire!
Break the third tape!

AUDIENCE PARTICIPANTS *for* SECOND BATTALION *follow* FURIES'S
*directions. There is the machine gun sound and the third tape is
broken and some fall to the ground. Blueout. Sound out. Snow sifts
down from above.*

HEPHAESTUS
Battle silence: at a certain moment everyone there in
Uritzky Square suddenly remembered the Sunday in 1905
when the Winter Palace had been last approached by the
people.

There is a very strange eerie music; FIRE, *as* FATHER GAPON *in*

priest's robe, appears from out of the Tunnel, moving toward the Hot
Spot, followed by others.

JULIAN

(as stage director)
Everyone on stage should lie down during this ...

FIRE AS GAPON

I, Father Capon, a priest, surrounded by carriers of icons
and pictures of the Czar, led a large crowd which moved
toward the Winter Palace by way of the Narva Gate. We
had come with a petition I had drawn up ...

FURIES

He had been a police spy who became convinced by the
role he was playing. Half mad and moved by the misery of
the people with whom he was working ...

FIRE

We came with a petition only, begging for bearable conditions; we were asking for the right to organize, the right
to eat; we did not seek the abdication of the Czar. O my
little brothers and sisters ...
(He sways in the center, his head in his hands.)

FURIES

(speaking softly)
It was a terrifying spectacle, a vision which could hardly be
imagined, unique in history. Machine-gunned point blank,
the immense crowd, unable either to advance or retreat
because its own size prevented all movement, was bathed
in blood. Hundreds of men, women, and children perished
... The number of victims was never known ... During
the night, long trains filled with corpses transported all
these poor bodies outside the city to be buried haphazardly
in fields and forests. And the Czar was not even in the
capital that day ...

CAPON *returns through the Tunnel.*

JULIAN
All right, you can get up now. Everybody resume your firing positions. Let's go on with the actual 1917 storming. Everybody, get ready to storm it!

FURIES/ZINOVIEV
Detachments of troops won over by the Bolsheviki blockaded the Palace. Take blockade positions! The infantry arrives. Infantry, march! Armored units arrived.

The AUDIENCE-INFANTRY *begins to march up the aisles: 1-2-3-hup, 1-2-3-hup and across the front of the stage; meanwhile the other* AUDIENCE-PLAYERS *have assumed blockade positions.*

FURIES
And at a quarter to twelve the battleship *Aurora* opened fire!
(BOOM, flash of red-orange in the Tunnel)
Break the fourth tape!

ZINOVIEV *and four audience* BOLSHEVIKI *rapidly cross the stage through the crowd and move toward the Winter Palace, taking it over.* FURIES/ZINOVIEV *and* HEPHAESTUS/MARTOV *mount to the top level of the Palace/Pyramid where they unfurl a large red banner and hang a luminous red star from the apex of the Pyramid. The other four* BOLSHEVIKI *mount the sides of Pyramid, two on each side, carrying each a red banner. As they do this,* ZINOVIEV *is speaking.*

FURIES *(continued)*
At 2:10 a.m. the guards of the Winter Palace surrendered. Break the fifth tape!
(As the fifth tape is cut the Pyramid is taken and "The Internationale" booms through the theatre.)
Everybody rise! Cross Uritzky Square. The Palace is ours! Kerensky has fled! The Provisional Government has fallen! Long live the Socialist World Revolution! All power to the Soviets!

The BOLSHEVIKI *repeat the slogans; all is celebration; lights on all over the theatre.*

FIRE

Proclaim your own liberty! Open the doors of all the prisons!

The people on stage have probably already begun to pull back the door of the Prison; the WOMEN *[audience participants] begin to come tentatively out and stand in front of the Pyramid, close together; they do not join in the festivities.*

FIRE

Dance in the streets!

("The Internationale" fades from its orchestral tone on the tape and is picked up by ORPHEUS, *playing it on the piano in a dance rhythm.)*

End the reign of the Czars
Open the gates of yourself
Let everyone in and out
End the era of closed doors
Open the doors of all the prisons
Open the question of equality again and again
Open the question of authority
Remember I am sent to eat out your mind

NARCISSUS

(standing in spotlight in the Orpheum on PANTHEA's *Mount)*
I am the question in your mirror
I see myself in the revolution
and I ask
does my love for myself
dissolve the law
of private property
(He moves among the people; lights slowly up.)
look at the revolution
it is a mirror of you

... now dream ...
(moves, looking into the eyes of individual spectators)

FURIES
(repeating; descending and returning to "Smolny" position stage left with other BOLSHEVIKS)
At 2:10 a.m.
the guards of the Palace surrendered.

KRUPSKAYA
A council of people's commissars was set up,
the chairman of which was Lenin.

LENIN
(at the lectern, speaking and moving in very tired watery slow motion; removing wig)
All power to the Soviets!

KRUPSKAYA
At four in the morning he went back to the apartment of
Bonch-Brucevich—where, at least, he was sure of a bed.

KRUPSKAYA *and* LENIN *begin very slowly to move across the stage.*

PROMETHEUS
(calling down)
Vladimir Ilyich,
if a worker has to work sixteen hours a day,
is he free?

LENIN
No, he's not free ...

PROMETHEUS
Vladimir Ilyich,
if a worker has to work eight hours a day,
is he free?

KRUPSKAYA
There was no entourage to accompany him ...

FIRE
(dropping a red cord)
Comrade,
*(*LENIN *looks up.)*
Comrade,
*(*LENIN *plays with the red thread.)*
what's this thing trailing you?

LENIN
(letting go of the cord)
What do you mean? It was an almost bloodless revolution ...

They move across the stage.

FURIES
The mass melted in the night.

The CHORUS *gives a long sigh.*

JULIAN
And the mass melted into the night ...
Thank you, you can go back to your seats now.

Scene 9: The Liberation of Metis

ORPHEUS
in the empty streets:
Scene Nine:

METIS *and the* WOMEN *in the prison have lighted candles.* PANTHEA *and four or more other women appear in the Tunnel with lighted candles. They fill out over the stage and move toward the audience. Tiny bells ring. They move the candles a little as in the glowing cities sequence at the end of Act I.*

METIS
(putting out her arm, holding the candle like the woman carrying the flame in the Guernica of Picasso)
this is the flame of utopia
it is coming out of the prisons and the cellars
out of the circumscribed circles

PANTHEA
in the streets
the generative flame of holy mother russia
begins to move

METIS
the match was hope
that lit the flames

PANTHEA
that walked the streets

As the WOMEN *move down the steps into the theatre, they blow out the candles and are absorbed into the spectators.*

METIS
that were built by men

PANTHEA
who put out the flame

METIS

inadvertently ...

(METIS *remains on stage, center, halfway toward the apron.*)

Lenin himself was acutely aware of our position. He issued decrees which invalidated the privileges of males over their dependents and affirmed the right of women to economic, social, and sexual self-determination; every legal provision was made for political and social equality: free marriage and divorce, contraception, and abortion on demand.

(*As she speaks,* LENIN *and* ZINOVIEV *are wrapping her in a red banner by drawing her in it to the right, pulling her to the lectern, carrying her over to the* CHORUS OF BOLSHEVIKS.)

Housekeeping was to be collectivized. Nurseries were established and women welcomed on an equal footing into the labor force.

(Millett, p. 229)

By this time, ZINOVIEV *has descended, holding one end of the red flag.* LENIN *remains on* METIS's *right, between her and Tunnel.*

FURIES/ZINOVIEV

(*softly, simply.*)

On November 20, 1920, incest, adultery, and homosexuality were dropped from the penal code.

ORPHEUS

Nothing was left out.

Nothing was forgotten.

EROS *appears in the Tunnel naked, with a flashlight taped to his thigh lighting his genitals and small lights at the joints of his body. Everything else is dark.*

EROS

Vladimir Ilyich,

don't forget me.

I'm waiting for an amnesty.

The jails are jammed

(reaches ladder and begins to climb)
and I want to get out.
Look at where I am; I'm in the confine zone.
Why do you avert your eyes?

LENIN
(crosses to right of Tunnel and paces back and forth in front of it)
The sexual revolution, like the social and sexual processes in general, is not adequately understood. Perhaps one day I shall speak or write on these questions, but not now. Now all our time must be dedicated to other matters.

EROS
But I am a gigantic force. You know that.

LENIN
I pass to the next question, that is ... the question of how to end the war.

EROS
I am the end of war.

LENIN
A war conducted by the capitalists of all countries against the workers of all these countries cannot be brought to a close without a workers' revolution against those capitalists. We Marxists do not belong to the unconditional enemies of all wars. There are wars and wars ...
(Fischer, p. 145)

LENIN *walks away toward center.*

EROS
The tribunals of the Soviets are passing laws to free me, but at the boutons of the brain the frontiers are fixed, and I am the passport ... I sign my name: Eros.

EROS, *during following, climbs and reaches Promontory, crosses it, and descends toward stage left.*

ZINOVIEV

(Crossing center; LENIN turns and comes back to meet him.)
Comrade Lenin, a letter from Comrade Piotr Kropotkin.

PROMETHEUS

(from on high)
Dear Vladimir Ilyich, *Izvestia* and *Pravda* have announced
that the Soviet Government has decided to take hostages
and, in case of attempts on the lives of Soviet leaders, to
execute these hostages without mercy. Is it possible that
there is no one among you to remind and persuade his
comrades that such measures contribute to a return to the
worst periods of the Middle Ages? They are unworthy of
people who have undertaken to build a future society on
communal lines, and cannot be employed by those who
hold dear the future of communism. At present, the Russian
Revolution is perpetrating horrors. It is ruining the whole
country. In its mad fury it is annihilating human lives. And
we are powerless for the present to direct it into another
channel, until such time as it will have played itself out.

LENIN *gives the letter back to* ZINOVIEV.

EROS

I'm climbing back into the night.
(He passes LENIN and disappears into Tunnel.)
I make veiled appearances from time to time.
Sometimes as an anarchist.
Sometimes as a Bolshevist.
(light down in Tunnel)

METIS/CLARA ZETKIN

Sometimes as a feminist.
(She begins to cross toward LENIN.)
Comrade Lenin discussed with me the problem of women's
rights.
*(They walk toward each other; he leads her upstage, arm around
her waist, and seats her in center of Octagon.)*

We had our first long talk on this subject in the autumn of 1920, in Lenin's big study in the Kremlin. His desk was covered with books and papers indicating study and work without the brilliant disorder associated with genius.

LENIN

(paces in circle)

I understand that in Hamburg a gifted communist woman is bringing out a newspaper for prostitutes. Now, some people might call this communist and even revolutionary, but aren't there industrial women in Germany who need organizing?

METIS

Before I could answer, he continued ...

LENIN

The record of your sins, Clara Zetkin, is even worse. I understand that at meetings organized by you, problems of sex and marriage are discussed first. Now, many people would call this revolutionary and communist, but I am an old man and do not like it; I may be a morose ascetic, but this so-called new sex life of young people seems to me purely bourgeois and simply an extension of the good old bourgeois brothel ...

(ZINOVIEV knocks, on the other side of the stage.)

I'm coming.

(He takes her hands and walks her down to top of steps.)

I'm going to take advantage of the fact that I was conversing with a woman and will blame the notorious female talkativeness as the excuse for being late ... You should dress more warmly.

(Memoirs of Clara Zetkin)

METIS

(walking up the aisle)

He shook my hand firmly.

SCENE 10: FEBRUARY 1921

ORPHEUS
Red is the poppy and the rose
is the eye of love
is the name of the radical activist
is the fire created by union
is the banner of the community of comrades
is the blood.

Scene 10:
February 1921.
The news.

The ANARCHISTS *dart around the theatre during the following.*

Furies/Zinoviev
Civil war.
*(*BOLSHEVIKS *repeat: "Civil war.")*
Economic dislocation.
*(*CHORUS: *"Civil war.")*
Sheer physical exhaustion of the population.
*(*CHORUS: *"Civil war.")*
Grave shortages of food and fuel.
*(*CHORUS: *"Civil war.")*
Strikes are sweeping Petrograd.
On February 24th the Committee of Defense
proclaimed a state of siege in Petrograd.
All circulation on the streets is forbidden after 11 p.m.
All meetings indoors and outdoors forbidden.
All infringements will be dealt with by military law.

Scene 11: Kronstadt

Orpheus
Scene 11: The Fire of Kronstadt.

Fire
Comrades of Kronstadt! Living conditions under the Communists leave us starved for both bread and freedom.

Panthea
We made the revolution so that workers could manage production themselves, so that peasants could own the land and work it as they see fit.

Eros
Now everyone in Russia is under the authority of the Bolsheviks. Where there is authority there is no freedom.

Fire
Strikes are sweeping Petrograd. We have sent people there to bring back news.

Panthea
Everyone to the meeting in Anchor Square!

The Anarchists *sweep down the aisle and onto the stage to address the entire audience.*

Hephaestus
(from the audience)
Comrades, we went to the factories in Petrograd. We drew up a program asking for the things we fought the revolution for. We asked for a free election of new soviets by secret ballot. We asked for the right to form our own workers' councils. For the rights of peasants to form their own organizations. For freedom of speech, freedom of assembly.

Fire
These demands have been refused.

PANTHEA

We declare Kronstadt a free Soviet, and invite all Russia to follow our example.

FIRE

Comrades of Kronstadt: Da or Njet? Are we united? Da or Njet?

The public responds. The ANARCHISTS *run into the aisles with flags, shouting, "Da! Daaaa!" and "Free Soviet! Free Soviet!"*

Scene 12: Moscow Radio

ORPHEUS
In the grammar of rhetoric
the structure of words defines the deed.

Scene 12.

KRUPSKAYA
Moscow Radio:

BOLSHEVIK CHORUS
Beep, beep, beep, beep ...
(The CHORUS *continues the high-pitched beep sound under* ZINOVIEV's *announcement.)*

ZINOVIEV
To the deceived people of Kronstadt! Lay down your arms and come over to us!

EROS
Kronstadt is the second Paris Commune!

LENIN
The time has come to put an end to opposition, to put the lid on it. We have had enough opposition.

PROMETHEUS
(from Promontory, in spotlight; rumbling of thunder, storm effects)
Let the pronged forks of lightning be launched at me.
Let the sound of thunder and the agony
of warring wind rack the sky.
Let the waves of the sea rise up and drown the stars.
Let him lift me high and hurl me to black Tartarus
on ruthless floods of irresistible doom.
I am the one he cannot kill.

BOLSHEVIK CHORUS
Beep, beep, beep ...
(continues under ZINOVIEV *and* TROTSKY*)*

ZINOVIEV
A radio message to the sailors of Kronstadt from the Petrograd Defense Committee signed by Comrade Trotsky.

TROTSKY
(recited by the actor who plays LENIN)
You are surrounded on all sides ...
If you insist we will shoot you like partridges.

ANARCHISTS
Free Soviet! Free Soviet!

PROMETHEUS
(calling down)
Stop! It will fail! The Kronstadt revolt is an old form.
Blood on snow
Russian dreams
Gravity defied
the confrontation of authority
Ghosts
Blood on snow
Snow against February
No. October sky.
I see it. I see it.
*(He has descended from the Promontory, comes forward, stage
center, and speaks directly to the public.)*
We will have to improvise. Something we can do very
quickly. Some kind of gesture or feeling—a configuration—
an emblem of the future wave. Here, why don't you people
in the front begin to come onto the stage, but crouched
low as if you were spilling onto it, your fingers spraying
toward the Bolsheviks like foam, like the fringe of the first
wave.
Behind you, the next five rows or so, a position something
like this,
(He demonstrates ...)
something magical, like magicians, palms open, to dispel

fear.

And the next few rows: the social impulse behind it. The weight of work felt in your shoulders, so. Yes, bent over a little, like that. But now, reach backwards or sideways, somehow or other touch one another, and look at one another. And everyone else—what shall we call it? The freedom impulse. Take any position you want, anything that feels free or that seems to you to express freedom. Embrace—you can do things together, and in groups. But quickly ... Good ... Now, hold still. Don't move. Shhhhh. Don't move. This is our emblem. This is our message.

(The public moving slowly forward, with a low hum.)

TROTSY/JULIAN

But you cannot change the course of history!

EMMA GOLDMAN *comes down the aisle to stage right. She crosses across front of stage to* LENIN/TROTSKY.

EMMA

(low, strong)

To keep silent now is impossible.

(She reads from a letter.)

The events of Kronstadt oblige us as anarchists to speak out. I've written a letter to the Petrograd Soviet: Comrades— the conflict at Kronstadt should be ended not by arms but by means of a revolutionary fraternal agreement. We should delegate a commission to go to Kronstadt to resolve the conflict by peaceful means. In the present situation it is the most radical solution. It will have international revolutionary importance. Signed Alexander Berkman and Emma Goldman. Petrograd, March 5th, 1921.

She and LENIN *are looking at each other, face to face; she gives him the letter.*

ZINOVIEV

March 8th, 1921, the Red Army opened fire.

The mutiny was suppressed within a week.
Shells exploded the ice. Thousands drowned.

Sound of shelling; red and white blitz lights sweep the audience.

JULIAN

Would you all lie down. Would everybody slump in their seats. You are all dead. The estimate is that 18,000 people were killed in Kronstadt. Now, play the dead.

After this action, LENIN returns to CHORUS position, stage left. Funereal music. A group of ANARCHISTS—FIRE, EROS, HEPHAESTUS, others—appear through the Tunnel carrying a black coffin and black flags. They cross stage right [Minsk]. EMMA falls behind the cortège.

BERKMAN/PROMETHEUS
(reclimbing)
Days of anguish and cannonading. Kronstadt has fallen.

EMMA

Only a month before, we had carried the black flag of anarchism through the streets of Moscow for Kropotkin's funeral. 20,000 people followed in the cortège.

She takes a flag.

BERKMAN

Grey days are passing now. One by one every ember of hope has died out.

As the cortège moves up the aisle, music changes. The sound of Tchaikovsky's "Marche Slav." Lights down except for reds in the auditorium and light in the audience left aisle. ISADORA DUNCAN in blue velvet scarves and a transparent trailing blue Grecian tunic appears, dancing slowly forward.

ISADORA

The posters read "Isadora Duncan and the Art of the Dance" when I first played in St. Petersburg. It was 1906, and I arrived just in time to see the night funeral of the marchers shot down in front of the Winter Palace. The murdering rulers of the world were not my people; the marchers were my people; the artist is not on the side of the machine gun ...

(Yesenin/Orpheus *opens champagne.*)

And when October split the husk off the old world, I remembered the coffins lurching through the streets, the white faces ... that night in Petrograd, and I danced the Marche Slav.

(Isadora *dances.*)

I danced back to Russia in 1922 ...

(*She and* Yesenin *toast, clink glasses, drink.*)

... full of hope for a school and work and a new life in freedom. I married the poet Sergei Yesenin.

Isadora *goes to Orpheum, where she kisses* Orpheus. *They drink champagne. While he recites, a bit drunkenly, she continues to dance, slowly, proceeding from movement to movement.*

Yesenin

Give me peace

(*drum and piano cacophony; calling across stage to* Lenin)

give me the love that plunges through bread

give me the delicious voice of the people

(*He plunges to* Lenin, *taking him by the lapels;* Lenin *gives him the rope.*)

give me crust and kernel

give me the dancing of an orchestra of clowns

(*to audience, in* Hot Spot, *with* Lenin)

rubies clashing in the opulence of freedom

give me give me give me

To Prometheus, *alone in the* Hot Spot, *in a spasm with the rope; he makes a gesture, hanging himself; then returns to music and Orpheum;* Isadora, *hand to mouth, stifles a scream.*

ZINOVIEV

(opening letter)

The poet Yesenin, initially enthusiastic about the revolution, but later disillusioned by industrialization ... wrote a farewell note in his own blood ... and hanged himself ...

ISADORA

I left Russia for the last time in 1925. I wrote Alexander Berkman from Nice.

(As she speaks, ISADORA dances up the aisle and out of the theatre.)

Dearest Sasha—You are woven in all my feelings and musings ... They are without food and fuel in Moscow. Do you know where has disappeared this "Miracle"? Dear Sasha, how I wish you could come here from Berlin. I've taken a studio by the sea and could give you a divan where you could recline and I would dance for you. You see, I am always ready to believe in a new "Myth" since the Bolshevik one didn't work out. I kiss you a thousand times. With all my love, Isadora.

She is up and out the rear aisle door of the theatre. Two shots are heard.

EMMA

(She turns back suddenly.)

Comrade Lenin! The Cheka has shot the anarchist poet Lev Chernyi and my friend Fanya Baron. I am so outraged that I considered making a scene in the manner of the English suffragettes by chaining myself in the hall where the Third Comintern is meeting ... Russian friends have dissuaded me.

She returns to cortège. Funeral music.

BERKMAN

Terror and despotism have crushed the life born in

140

October. The breath of yesterday is dooming millions. The revolution is dead ... I have decided to leave Russia.

EMMA

I spoke at Kropotkin's graveside.

(She is in aisle.)

And I remembered what the old man had said: "anarchism stands for the liberation of the human mind ... prison and all punishment is an abomination which should be done away with for all time."

(She and the cortège begin to move out.)

Braving the bitter cold of the Moscow winter, the cortège carried the body to the Navodevichii burial ground. That was the last time the black flag was carried through the streets of Moscow.

Funeral music continues. LENIN's *rigid body is picked up and carried by* FURIES/ZINOVIEV *and three others toward the Pyramid.* KRUPSKAYA *follows.*

KRUPSKAYA

Lenin's body was brought to Moscow on January 23, 1924. He had died two days before. The city fell into deep mourning. Hundreds of thousands of people, men and women and children, formed long lines for hours in the bitter cold, waiting to file past the body. The body lay in state for four days in the Hall of Columns. Later the body was taken to a laboratory, his organs and body fluids removed, and preservative liquids substituted. Friends have reported that I opposed his mummification, and it is not difficult to understand the emotional reason.

(Fischer, p. 674)

LENIN's *body is placed in state on the top level of the Pyramid, standing up at a slant between the tripods of* ZEUS, *which are relighted. A rose is placed in his hand.* KRUPSKAYA *goes to the prison below and writes her memoirs.*

ORPHEUS *begins to move across the stage with Orpheus Screen used to introduce the Oriental Theatre scene, moving from stage left to stage right, toward the Orpheum. Lights change to rich yellows, blue, and green—as at the entrance of* ORPHEUS *in the first act. As he moves across the stage, the actoresses come into place for the Circus Play.* EROS, FIRE, HEPHAESTUS, PANTHEA, *all the people of the House of the Creative. The pallbearers have descended from the Pyramid. The* BOLSHEVIK CHORUS *returns to its place stage left, with* ZINOVIEV.

ORPHEUS
> *(moving with screen)*
> It is all an emotional reason
> the tumult of mountains is a reason
> the love of strangers another
> another is April 1930:

> At the Moscow State Circus:
> we present:
> 1905 "Moscow Is Burning"
> a play by
> Vladimir Mayakovsky.

Screen goes offstage. ORPHEUS *reaches Orpheum and begins to play circus music. A constructivist octagonal screen has been placed upright in the middle of the stage. Before it are at least eight actoresses who have taken costumes from under the Pyramid and elsewhere and move with a machine movement in a machine rhythm. It is biomechanical. As the machine moves, the poet plays and recites/sings:*

ORPHEUS
> Fan
>   the collective
>   bellows of your lungs
> Rush this slogan
>   through the working teams
> from shock brigades
>   to shock shops

from the shops
> to shock factories

Breathing
> with their entire
> > chests

Yelling with happy mouths
The Five Year Plan

CIRCUS PERFORMERS
> Forward!
> > Forward!
> > > Forward!

The music and the actoresses reach a climax. ORPHEUS *rises and bows. Actoresses break their positions and bow. Applause. They now form individual machines about the stage.* ORPHEUS *and* ZINOVIEV *form one downstage center.*

ORPHEUS
> Star of the soviets
> > shine over the world

> whatever happens
> > the enemy feet

> won't step
> > on our lands

> Comrade
> > through your laughter
> > look and learn

> to hate the enemy
> > to the bottom of your heart

Climax of movement/music. ORPHEUS *held aloft. All bow.* ORPHEUS *and* ZINOVIEV *go to positions at bottom of ladders. During the next lines they climb in blackouts toward Rock. The actoresses take the octagonal screen, thrusting faces, hands, feet through a hole in the center. Two stand in the center of it [behind] and two or more on each side. The effect should be two-dimensional. The lights flash on and off and the actoresses make tableaux vivants. Each time the lights come on,* ORPHEUS *and* ZINOVIEV *are higher and higher on the ladders. They speak when the lights are on.* ZINOVIEV *is in ecstasy;* ORPHEUS/MAYAKOVSKY *is in anger.*

ZINOVIEV
Listen to me behind silence

MAYAKOVSKY
Listen to me over silence

ZINOVIEV
poems lie in the snow

MAYAKOFSKY
(anguished)
like a bright chill

ZINOVIEV
A poem is a mirror reflecting utopia

MAYAKOVSKY
This is our last
and decisive battle

ZINOVIEV
When you write, you must press your hand against eternity.

In the blackout ZINOVIEV *shoots* MAYAKOVSKY, *who, when the lights come up, slumps dead. They are both at the highest point of the ladders.)*

ZINOVIEV
(pulling out a telegram)
My god! This morning, the poet Comrade Vladimir Mayakovsky committed suicide!

Wind sound, lights down except on PROMETHEUS.

PROMETHEUS
An end to words. Deeds now.
The world is shaken.
Deep and secret thunder roars.

Fiery wreaths of lightning flash. Holocaust.
Whirlwinds toss swirling dust. Asphyxiation!
O Mother Earth, O sun and moon
Whose light is everyone's,
You see how I am wronged!

BLACKOUT /CURTAIN

INTERLUDE

ACT III

PROMETHEUS UNBOUND
THE REALITY

As the curtain rises the actoresses are arranged in an arc across the arch of the structure—ladder, Promontory, ladder—dressed in the colors of the rainbow. At the foot of the ladders are their coats and bags and whatever paraphernalia they usually carry when they are out on the street.

ORPHEUS
(He strikes a cymbal.)
An end to words.
Act III
Prometheus Unbound
A silent action.
A silent walk.
The scene:
is/will be the Piazza Comunale
(or whatever place is chosen for this night's action)
in front of the jail
of the Questura of Prato
(or name of jail for this night)
a silent vigil
a mass action
to be done with your participation
a silent march together
with stars and lights
a silent vigil
with light and a fire sermon wordless
of one half hour
(In some cases ten minutes; here are given details about how to arrive at the prison, by car or by foot, etc.)

146

And there in front of the prison the play will end.
Now the safety of the theatre begins to end.
The arc dissolves. The actors and actresses descend.
The lights will fade to blackout. The actors and actresses
will bow and then melt into the night to meet at the prison
and there perform an act of meditation, a silent vigil
in the name
of the end
of punishment.

The actoresses begin to descend from the arc, take up their things, put on their coats, and file out of the theatre slowly. ORPHEUS *plays the postlude. If the police do not grant permission for the vigil,* ORPHEUS *announces after the last line that permission has been refused and lists all the places where it has taken place in the past. As he speaks this, the actoresses walk slowly backwards into the Tunnel. Then a regular curtain call.*

APPENDIX A

SOURCES FOR 'PROMETHEUS'

Many of the words spoken in this production are quotations from the following authors:

ACT I

Aeschylus	Simone Weil	Paul Goodman
Shelley	W. C. Williams	Heidegger
Hesiod	Schopenhauer	Nietzsche
Marcuse	Pound	Gandhi
Wollstonecraft	Bhagwan Shree Rajneesh	

Julian Beck and Judith Malina: *We the Living Theatre*

ACT II

1. Bolshevism

Fischer, Louis: *The Life of Lenin,* New York, 1964 (Harper Colophon Books)

Lenin, Vladimir I.: *What Is To Be Done?*, New York, 1929 (International Publishers Co. Inc.)

Lenin, Vladimir I.: *State And Revolution,* New York, 1929 (International Publishers Co. Inc.)

Lenin, Vladimir I.: *"Left Wing" Communism, an Infantile Disorder,* Peking, 1965 (Foreign Languages Press)

Ulam, Adam B.: *Lenin and the Bolsheviks,* London/Glasgow, 1966 (The Fontana Library)

Carr, Edward Hallett: *The Boshevik Revolution 1917-1923,* Harmondsworth, 1966 (Penguin Books)

Wilson, Edmund: *To the Finland Station,* New York, 1953 (Doubleday Anchor Books)

Trotsky, Leon: *My Life,* Harmondsworth, 1975 (Penguin Books)

2. Anarchism

Arshinov, Peter: *History of the Makhnovist Movement,* Detroit/ Chicago, 1974 (Solidarity/Black and Red)

Avrich, Paul (Ed.): *The Anarchists in the Russian Revolution,* New York, 1973 (Cornell Paperbacks)

Avrich, Paul: *The Russian Anarchists,* Princeton, 1967 (Princeton University Press)177

Guerin, Daniel: *L'anarchisme,* Paris, 1965 (Editions Gallimard)

Horowitz, Irving Louis (Ed.): *The Anarchists,* New York, 1964 (The Universal Library, Grosset & Dunlap)

La Commune de Cronstadt—Recueil de documents comprenant la traduction integrale des Izvestias de Cronstadt, Paris, 1969 (Bélibaste)

Mett, Ida: *The Kronstadt Uprising,* Montreal, 1971 (Black Rose Books)

Voline: *The Unknown Revolution,* Detroit/Chicago, 1974 (Solidarity/Black & Red)

Woodcock, George: *Anarchism,* Harmondsworth, 1963 (Pelican Books)

3. Leo Tolstoy

Tolstoy, Leo: *The Slavery of Our Times* (1900), New York (Unity Press)

Tolstoy, Leo: *On Civil Disobedience and Non-Violence,* New York, 1967 (Mentor Books)

4. Magazines

The Drama Review (Ed. Michael Kirby), Volume 17, No. 1,

New York, March 1973

Deak, Frantisek: "Russian Mass Spectacles," *The Drama Review* (Ed.: Michael Kirby), Volume 19, No. 2, New York, 1975

5. Biographical Material, Letters

Richard and Anna Maria Drinnon (Ed.): *Nowhere at Home— Letters from Exile of Emma Goldman and Alexander Berkman*, New York, 1975 (Schocken Books)

Richard Drinnon (Ed.): *Rebel in Paradise—a biography of Emma Goldman*, Chicago, 1961 (Harper Colophon Books)

Kate Millett: *Sexual Politics*, New York, 1969 (Avon Books)

6.

John Dos Passos: *U.S.A.*, New York, 1930 (1966, Penguin Books)

Appendix B

Prometheus
Program/Synopsis

Act I

The Prologue in the Theatre
we are bound to the past

The Prologue Onstage
we speak and move in the cycle of our recent history
"we have to face once again all the issues ...
which have been with the Living Theatre
since the very beginning"

The House of the Creative
Panthea draws a straight line
the principles of Euclid
Drawn by her mathematics, Orpheus emerges
singing the colors of light
Hephaestus and Eros, form and feeling, bear Orpheus aloft
Hephaestus animates the Dream Machine
Panthea disarms Eros
"why do you hunt?"
Orpheus invokes the myth
"the scene is a desolate landscape
enter ... Prometheus"

Prometheus the Firebringer
gives us his gifts
Power and Force bind him
with Aeschylus's words
"We have come to the end of the earth"
he cries out
"everyone is harsh who comes to power"

The Poet and Prometheus
they hear, respond and speak
"the mechanisms have started their racket"
the imagination takes flight
a bird draws a thread of sky
across the empty space between performer and public

The Myth Chorus
an image – fixed, moving
"the marble hand at the beginning of time"

The Encounters of Prometheus
he foretells the uses of fire
invention – physical, psychic, social
"will not your movement lead to violence, Mahatma?"
the snows of Russia

Fire and Prometheus
burn and are not consumed
summon the enquiry of science

The Doctors Chorus
Aeschylus: "though they had eyes to see"
Pythagoras: "from the pyramid, arose fire"
Zeus leads
he holds the brain
divided by the Furies
witnessed in Narcissus's mirror
five solids
the illuminated mind perceives structure

The Titans
Prometheus's trick – meat, fat, bones, sacrifice
Zeus hurls Prometheus from the company of the gods
"never to give the power of fire to humankind"
the dodecahedron atop the pyramid
borne by the new master of heaven

Metis's Vision of the Skies

Galilea

suppression of the women's wisdom with the coded cloth
the swallowing of Metis: prison – she lives in Zeus's belly
the burning glass – the secret of the spark

The Fire Wheel

"the sun's eye is a burning glass"
the original light
Shabbos

Promethea

chooses the role of the consort Hera
the washerwomen at the well wash Hera's veil
Egyptian words
Zeus sees through Metis's telescope, the devout Io
the arrow of Eros
the commission of Hera to Orpheus
"there is a story of a woman transformed into a cow
I want to hear it now"

The Ritual of Oriental Theatre

Orpheus transforms the stage
"a philosopher king under a banyan
a priestess in a pasture
an empress in a pavilion"
the enlightenment of Chiyono: no moon
Kung walks: spreading order
"history has come to be out of control"
the empress calls upon the magician, Hermes
the transformation of Io into a cow
Hermes Oceanus the masks of god
the mask of Hera

Io Pursued by the Furies

the questions of Prometheus
Wittgenstein, Schopenhauer, and Simone Weil on suffering
caught by the imagination

How Can We End Human suffering?
the tableau of the Delphic oracle
the tableau of the creation of Pandora
the stoning of Dionysus
the visions of Narcissus's mirror
the tableau of women adored
the gift of the gods
Pandora's box

Fourteen Box Plays: Light and Heat
Pandora – The Deadly Female Race
Zeus – The Origin of the Laws of Thermodynamics
Fire – The Question of the Use of Energy
Hera – Several Faces – Lilith, Eve, Hera, Promethea
Prometheus – The Accidental Adam, The Accidental Eve
Orpheus – Hell
Furies – So Many Stones
Hephaestus – Dream Machines, War Machines
Panthea – Nourishment and Slaughter
Eros – Love's Dart
Narcissus – Metamorphosis Floral
Metis – Death and Life in Jail
Io – Who Will Pay My Bills?
    "the light bill and the gas bill … "

The Fire Theft
    "that which is left behind is not stolen …
    he hid it in a fennel stalk"
the cities glow
the rage of Zeus
the binding of Prometheus by Hephaestus
    "take him out of the city"
the Furies rage
    "what are we going to do with our capacity
    to decipher the burning signs?"
we are bound to the past
the next act: out of the tunnel

INTERLUDE

ACT II

The Train and the Ship
    April 1917 – a sealed train
    "finally, finally, finally, finally"
    Lenin, Krupskaya, and the Bolsheviks enter Russia

January 1920
    Emma Goldman and Alexander Berkman aboard ship
    with 51 other anarchists deported from America to Russia
    Finland Station
    1917 – the arrival of Lenin
    1920 – the arrival of Emma Goldman and Alexander Berkman
    Interview: Lenin, Goldman and Berkman

    "why are anarchists here in Russia being kept in prison?"
    "free speech is a bourgeois luxury"

    disillusionment

The Storming of the Winter Palace
    the director – Lenin/Julian Beck sets the stage
    organization of audience participants:
        1) Red Guard and People's Brigade
        2) Narodniks = Terrorists
        3) Bolsheviks
        4) Anarchists
        5) Tolstoyan pacifists
        6) Women
        7) Mayakovsky's troupe
    the rehearsals for the assault
    workshops with audience participants

    Orpheus narrates the Historical Play
    everyone plays their part

Scene 1: March 1898, Minsk
the founding of the Communist Party
the Bolsheviks
Lenin and Iskra

Scene 2: Petrograd, March 1, 1881
terrorist action
assassination of Czar Alexander II
by Narodnaya Volya – The People's Will

Scene 3: Moscow, 1892
the anarcho-syndicalists rehearsing the Great Play
"is there something moving underfoot?"

Scene 4: Odessa, 1895
a group of Tolstoyans scything the wheat
the Song of the Wheat
the confrontation of the pacifists and the terrorists

Scene 5: Petrograd
the arrest of Alexander Ulyanov, Lenin's brother
the plot against the life of Czar Alexander III

Scene 6: February, 1917
the second storm
strikes in Petrograd, mutinies
the Provisional Government of Kerensky
factory organization
Prometheus's warning

Scene 7: July, 1917
the July days
Lenin in a wig hiding
Emma Goldman challenges Lenin
"how long do you foresee this transition period will be?"
Lenin returns to Petrograd – October
armed insurrection

Scene 8: October 25, 1917
the storming of the Winter Palace
Trotsky declares the end of the Provisional Government
distribution of guns and ammunition
setting the tapes:
> first tape – attack by armed workers
> "an unknown number fell"
> second tape – attack by Red Army
> "spilling blood"
> third tape – attack by Second Battalion
> "battle silence"
> Father Gapon and the countless dead in Uritsky Square
> "machine-gunned point blank ... bathed in blood"
> fourth tape – infantry arrives
> battleship Aurora
> fifth tape – taking of the Winter Palace
> Narcissus questions us
the aftermath
Lenin tired
"an almost bloodless revolution"

Scene 9: the liberation of Metis
the women emerge with light
short-lived freedom
repeal of abusive laws
against women
against sexual liberty
Lenin and Eros
"I am the end of war"
Kropotkin/Prometheus's warning
Clara Zerkin, a founder of the German Communist Party,
> hears Lenin's view of free love
> "an extension of the good old bourgeois brothel"

Scene 10: February, 1921
civil war
strikes, prohibitions

Scene 11: Kronstadt
anarchist meetings
the sailors and the factory workers
a free soviet

Scene 12: Moscow Radio
"people of Kronstadt, lay down your arms"
Lenin – "we have had enough opposition"
Prometheus – "irresistible doom"
Trotsky – "we will shoot you like partridges"
Prometheus – "old forms"
Emma Goldman and Alexander (Sasha) Berkman's letter
   to the Petrograd Soviet
      "a revolutionary fraternal agreement"
March 8, 1921 – 18,000 dead in Kronstadt
the funeral procession of Kropotkin
Isadora Duncan dances in Russia
the Marche Slav
as the coffins of the martyrs of 1905 pass
   "the marchers were my people"
the marriage and death of the poet Sergei Essenin
Isadora's love letter to Sasha
   "I am ready for a new myth
   since the Bolshevik one didn't turn out"
the death of Fanya Baron and Lev Cernyi
   "the last time the black flag was carried through
   the streets of Moscow"
the funeral of Lenin
the mummification
the Moscow State Circus
a scene from "1905 - Moscow Is Burning"
by Vladimir Mayakovsky

159

with biomechanics
the Poet and the Party
   "press your hand against eternity"
suicide
Prometheus
   "an end to words deeds now"

INTERLUDE

ACT III

the question is:
for what crime, if any, are we being punished
when we are being punished?

Appendix C

Prometheus
Record of Performances

1978

Sept. 24	Prato	Teatro Metastasio & Piazza degli Innocenti	1/900
Sept. 25, 26	Prato	Teatro Metastasio & Piazza delle Carceri	2/1,700
Sept. 30, Oct. 1-3	Roma	Teatro Argentina & in front ofRegina Coelli	4/4,800
Oct. 9-13	Dublin	Olympia Theatre & in front of Bridwell Prison; Ministry of Justice, Stephen's Green (Oct. 11)	5/1,100
Nov. 7, 9	Amiens	Maison de Ia Culture	2/1,200
Nov. 15-18	Lillc	Salle Municipal Roger Salengro	4/1,400
Nov. 21	Esch-sur-Alzette	Théâtre Municipal	1/800
Dec. 6-9	Bruxelles	Théâtre 140	4/1,600
Dec. 11, 12	Liège	Foyer du Culture! du Sart-Tilman a l'Université de Liège	2/350

1979

Feb. 21	Treviso	Teatro Comunale	1/900
Mar. 3, 4, 5	Mantova	Teatro Antonio Galli Bibiena	4/2,200
Mar. 12, 13	Udine	Teatro delle Mostre	2/1,000
Mar. 17. 18	Padova	Teatro Verdi	2/1,000
Mar. 20	Adria	Teatro Comunale del Popolo	1/600

Mar. 23-25	Trieste	Teatro Stabile al Teatro Auditorium	3/1,800
Apr. 10-14	Milano	Palazzina Liberty (Pza. Marinai d'Italia)	5/1,000
Apr. 18	Ferrara	Teatro Comunale	1/400
Apr. 22	Ravenna	Teatro Rasi	1/550
Apr. 28-30	Parma	Teatro Regio	3/1,500
Mav 10-13	Bologna	Teatro Eleanora Duse	4/2,500
July 9-28	London	The Round House	17/2,000
Oct. 22	Salonika	National Theatre	1/1,000
Nov. 2-5	Piraeus	People's Theatre	5/3,200

Prometheus was performed a total of 75 times. The site for the vigil is listed only through the Dublin engagement. Vigils took place after every performance (except for a few times when they were forbidden) in front of the nearest prison; if a prison was not available, an appropriate law enforcement edifice was used.

Appendix D

Act III
(first version, never used)

The objective of Act III is to bring about not only the symbolic liberation of Prometheus, but to stimulate utopian visions among the public, to open up the possibilities of the public's own Promethean foresight, and to bring the public and all of us closer to existential sensations of freedom. This is to be accomplished through the performance of a series of ritual actions.

Notes and Instructions

The Liberation of Prometheus. The conditions for the liberation are the accomplishment of five rituals. The five rituals should be prompted by the reactions of the members of the public, but we can instruct ourselves as follows:

if they are silent, we enact what is imprisoned in the mind.

if they are hostile, we fulfill our function as servants of the dream and move ahead to the next vision.

if they are irrelevant, we return to what is relevant, avoiding hostility.

if they are relevant, we try to incorporate them in the ritual.

The conditions for the liberation of Prometheus:

1. The liberation of women, and consequently men, from the impulses of the male-dominated culture with its violent response mechanisms.

2. The rebirth, or revival, of the imagination, the liberation of the imagination. The last murder will occur the last

time that we have killed the imagination or have killed the possibility of imagining other solutions to hostile or violent responses in the mind.

3. The liberation of Eros, leading to the eroticization of life and politics, the consequent liberation of love and concern for the human body, life.

4. The healing of the divided brain leading to the transformation of the Furies into their opposite – Demogorgon and the Orphic defeat of death.

5. The transformations of the Furies, making it possible for both Prometheus and Zeus to be free of all desire for vengeance and belief in punishment, making possible the capacity to forget, understood by both Shelley and Marcuse as essential for the liberation of us all. But it is also our capacity to remember our humanness which creates the ground for reconciliation. The result of the liberation is the freeing of utopian visions, of foresight, and the implications of their fulfillment.

Sound of wind. Curtain. Lights up. The actoresses are looking at the dead body of EROS *(as in Act I).* THE WINGS *also lies dead, where he was at the end of Act II.[1]* PROMETHEUS *is bound to the rock.* METIS *is in prison. The actoresses move slowly forward, peering out into the audience, gazing, like* PROMETHEUS, *out at the lone and ghastly landscape of Scythia.*

Io
  What land is this,
  What people,
  What crime have you committed that as penalty
  you are doomed to destruction?

FURIES
  Immobile … tied in knots …

---

1 The character of THE WINGS was cut from the final version of the play

HEPHAESTUS
We have come to the end of the earth.

Everyone falls suddenly to the ground as in the Issues Chorus, and rises, supporting themselves on the palms of their hands.

CHORUS
We want to act out your visions

PROMETHEUS
There is a story about the Liberation of Prometheus.
I want to hear it now!

CHORUS
In the theatre of dreams
we, the performers, the living, are the shadows;
Light us up: you are the fire.

The actressors swivel into sitting positions and scan the audience slowly with eyes and hands as if they were a kind of radar instrument.

PROMETHEA
Give us the cue.

ORPHEUS
Tell us the story.

The actoresses remain gazing at the public for one minute without changing their position or action. When there are silent waits, and at other points, the tapes of our discussions and readings can be heard. This opening passage is perhaps the same passage that was heard at the opening of the play.

NOTE ON THE ACTIONS: *The actions should all have the quality of the gentle. The movements should be ultimately resolved in softness. The movements should be generally slow, and tho there may be sudden or rapid gestures, the essential resolution is always peaceful.*

ACTION I

THE WOMEN *rise facing the audience. They pull* THE MEN *to their feet.*

PANTHEA

The story has many parts.

PANDORA

Five are essential.

METIS

(stepping out of the prison and coming forward)
All concern women.

THE WOMEN *move toward the public in the theatre space. When they get to the aisles [two in one aisle, three in the other] they each reach out a hand to a man and pull him to his feet in the aisle. They execute the biomechanics of a Meyerhold slap in the face [or other sudden sharp movement etude]: that is, they slap their hands twice and then lean backwards and come forward with an upraised hand, but hold back before the moment of contact. The actoresses should feel their own fear and hostility and whatever anger or hate they feel, and then consciously turn the hate into energy which makes it possible to ask the questions and to proceed with the ritual of touch. As their hands are poised in the air, they ask:*

THE WOMEN

Are you afraid of the violence inside yourself?
(a moment of waiting)
Are you afraid of the violence in me?
(The fingers of both their hands begin dancing and slowly approaching the subject of the ritual.)
Are you afraid of my fingers?
(They begin to let their fingers dance lightly over his face, forehead, body.)
Is there something to fear?
(They repeat the action with other people. The actors come down from the stage now and repeat the same action with other spectators.)

166

The sound of THE WOMEN'*s voices asking the four questions is heard blending in with the tape. At the end of this ritual there is a sound like an avalanche.* PROMETHEUS *cries out:*

PROMETHEUS

This ice melts! Listen!
The sun-awakened avalanche!
As thought by thought is piled
In heaven-defying minds till some great truth
Is loosened, and the nations echo round
Shaken to their roots, so do the mountains now.

IO

(in the aisle)
"Look how the gusty sea of mist is breaking
in crimson foam, the foam of dawn! it rises
As Ocean at the enchantment of the moon
Round foodless men wrecked on some oozy aisle ... "
(Prometheus Unbound II, 3, 37-47)

ACTION II

The CHORUS *makes a choral hum or other sound.*

PANDORA

(to audience)
You are the oracle

ORPHEUS

Don't read the Tarot

PANTHEA

Don't study the zodiac

NARCISSUS

Like the ancients who looked into the entrails of birds,

ZEUS

But tell me, what do you imagine when you dream of the future?

CHORUS
  (ad lib)
  Tell me …

TAPE

The tape is about visions. The actoresses wait one minute for the public to respond. During Action I both EROS *and* THE WINGS *have begun slightly to stir,* THE WINGS *moving its elbows while remaining in prone positions.* THE WINGS *rises; there's a signal sound on the* TAPE *and* THE WINGS *speaks.*

THE WINGS: THE STORY OF THE LAST MURDER

As he speaks, he moves from the stage space into the theatre and takes someone by the hand. As he moves with the person, if possible, he looks him/her in the eye and makes body contact with him/her. he takes a mudra-of-imagination position. The other actoresses do the same as he speaks.

THE WINGS
  The mind imagines
  – what is it? –
  a color we have never seen?
  or harmonic timelessness?
  eternity?
  When the imagination stops – pahhhhh –
  *(*WINGS *and the other actoresses fall suddenly to the ground where they stand and slowly rise again.)*
  It rises again.
  (They all rise and go to another audience member.)
  The mind imagines
  that all the jails of the body open,
  and the image is suppressed – pahhhh –
  *(*ALL *fall.)*
  and rises again …
  The imagination
  imagines the last murder

*(The actors have moved to the next person; the ritual forms can be
created with two or even three spectators at a time.)*
and dies – pahhhh –
(ALL fall.)
and rises again
the mind imagines
a theatre full of utopian visionaries
and the dream is called impossible – pahhhh –
(ALL fall; ALL rise.)
and rises again
The actoresses begin to move toward the stage space.

PROMETHEUS
And we will search with looks and words of love
For hidden thoughts, each lovelier than the last ...
weave harmonies divine ...
From difference sweet where discord cannot be ...

ACTION III

*EROS has begun to stir more and more as the imagination has
repeatedly reasserted itself.*

EROS
(rising slowly, moving toward the Orpheum)
When you imagine love in liberty
Do you feel it in the ends of your hair,
in your toes and elbows,
in all the crannies of the mind?
Imagine also politics eroticized and love in all its crannies ...

*EROS begins to play on the saxophone. PANTHEA joins him in the
Orpheum. The others have begun to move together in an Orgone
Movement. PANTHEA strikes the gong. They take love positions. As
they return to the center, two or three of the actoresses beckon to the
public to come and join them. This continues for four or five gongs.*

TAPE

Tape discussons on x y z plus loops. After three minutes PROMETHEUS
is heard.

PROMETHEUS

In the story of Prometheus
when does the Herculean labor
to liberate him end,
when does the effort collect
flake by flake
until it crashes through the rock?
(Pause thirty seconds)
When?

ACTION IV

NARCISSUS *takes someone from among the audience members on
the stage, or if no audience members are on stage, from the seated
audience, and leads the person toward the brain on one side of the
proscenium.*

NARCISSUS

When? When the half moon joins the half moon

*The music fades away and all of the actoresses begin to move in two
groups toward the divided brain halves.*

PANDORA

(leading the second group)
When? When Eros and Order are not worlds apart ...

ORPHEUS

When death is no longer accepted as fate.

PROMETHEA

When what is male in me
and female in me unite
to make me Promethea

THE OTHERS

(as they take the brain parts and move toward one another)

170

Careful …
Careful …

The procession moves around the theatre and begins perhaps to make a humming sound. One group perhaps moves weaving through the seats to avoid meeting the other group until they meet, in the theatre if there is space, on stage if there is not.

FIRE
(as the processions move around)
When two processions curving
like two currents of air
bring toward one another
the energy of east and west
(processions approaching each other cautiously)
moving toward each other
after so many years of exile from each other
like two nerves swimming toward each other
drawn like the two elements of love
become one –

The brain meets and clamps together in the hands of FURIES/ DEMOGORGON *who makes an ecstatic sound.* ZEUS *begins climbing to the Promontory.*

PROMETHEUS
Synapse! Synapto!
Clasp tightly!
Freely feeling
what has so long been
numb

The actoresses clasp a spectator. Lean backwards. Clasp them again in warm embrace and whisper:

ACTORESSES
The promise of this embrace is Utopia.

The action is repeated for two minutes.

DEMOGORGON
(standing in the Hot Spot with the brain in his hands, moving)
It is like a crystal ball.
It contains the capacity to imagine
what has never been
the capacity to hope
and to change
the Furies into their opposite
and to go from this domain of theatre
toward the theatre beyond these walls

He moves down the aisle toward the street. He moves very very slowly until the end of the play, when he moves out with the public into the foyer and with them into the street, speaking with them freely.

ZEUS *and* PROMETHEUS *meet on the Promontory.* ZEUS *begins to unbind* PROMETHEUS.

PROMETHEUS
It contains the capacity to forget. What did I say?

PROMETHEA
(calling up)
You said, "Shall Zeus one day be hurled from his domain?"

PROMETHEUS
Were these my words? A curse?
Words are quick and vain …
I wish no living thing to suffer pain …

He and ZEUS *on the Promontory reverse positions.*

IO
(from below)
Do you remember the word punishment?

PROMETHEUS
(pulling ZEUS from the rock)
Punishment? I hardly remember what it is
just as I cannot remember the reality of an age of cannibalism.

ZEUS
(descending)
You forget. My brain remembers a time
when there was a world of punishment, of masters and
slaves
and though my mind imagines it
it seems to me impossible
as impossible as utopian visions seemed long ago
which I now begin to see ...

He reaches the ground and peers out into the theatre space.)

PANTHEA
What do you see?

Wait, freeze, one minute. Then ORPHEUS *comes singing through
the Tunnel. He comes dancing out with a silver skeleton, or with a
skull mounted on scarecrow sticks. As he dances into the Hot Spot,*
PROMETHEA *begins to move with him. They move into the audience
space and circle back toward the stage, dancing and singing.*

ORPHEUS
(singing, repeating)
I sing
   the end of death
   the dancing end of death

I sing
   the end
I sing
   the end
I sing
   the end of death

I sing
   the end of death
   the dancing end of death
I sing the dance
I sing the dance

173

I dance the end of death
I dance the end of death
I sing and I dance
I sing and I dance
I sing the end of death ...

PROMETHEUS *comes to the edge of the stage, the Hot Spot, with* Io, *with all the actoresses,* ORPHEUS *still dancing in the theatre,* DEMOGORGON *moving toward the street; he stands in the Hot Spot.*

PROMETHEUS
I see it out there
as in glowing ciphers over your heads,
emerging right out of you:
"Only utopia frees.
Anything less will enslave us."

Io
(looking out in wonder)
What land is this?
What people?
What have they done
that they should gleam
with so much beauty?

The actoresses are gazing with wonder at the public. Lights down. Curtain?

THE ARCHAEOLOGY OF SLEEP

FOREWORD
by Tom Walker

Julian Beck wrote *The Archaeology of Sleep* in 1983, when The Living Theatre was in residency in Nantes, France. The Living had resided in Rome for the previous six years. When Jack Lang, the French minister of culture, offered the residency to create a new work, the company decamped to Brittany for four months. Unfortunately, it coincided with the onset of Julian's cancer, which would take him two years later. Before he entered the clinic, he treated us to what would be his last play, in a delightful reading of his finished work as we sat in the Salle Paul Fort, where we would open the play in June.

Judith directed the production. Julian, weak and wan after his surgery, was able to supervise the lighting as he reclined on a couch. The work (performed in French) was greeted by the public enthusiastically. We were all rewarded with a tremendous collective creation led by Julian, who had begun to think of the work years before, influenced by *The Archaeology of Knowledge* by his friend Michel Foucault.

Parallel to the opening of the play was the *Museum of Sleep* at the Maison de la Culture, where Living Theatre members collaborated with local artists to create works on the theme of sleep: dances, theatre pieces, art works, poetry from local students, and installations. Christian Vollmer and I recreated the death of Jacques Vaché, a surrealist hero to André Breton. Vaché died in the Hotel de France in Nantes in January 1919 from an overdose of opium, naked in bed with another young soldier. Christian and I approached a bed in the atrium of the Maison exhibit, in the bright sunlight of an early afternoon, surrounded by public. We undressed, slipped under the covers, and "slept." We had opium paraphernalia beside the bed, and a notice from the Nantes newspaper of the period, explaining the permanent "sleep" of Vaché. After two hours, we emerged, dressed, and walked away. We felt perfectly in tune with the dada of Julian's play.

After the run of *The Archaeology of Sleep* in Nantes, Julian sadly told us his cancer had metastasized and that he and Judith had decided to disband the Living for the time being to take stock.

Two months later Francis Ford Coppola cast Julian in *The Cotton Club,* and Julian decided to reunite the company in New York for a run at the Joyce Theater. He spent much of his Hollywood pay on producing the run. We performed four plays in repertory: *Antigone* (1967, revived 1979); *The One and the Many* (1980), the 1920 German Expressionist play by Ernst Toller; *The Yellow Methuselah* (1982) by Hanon Reznikov, based on Shaw's *Back to Methuselah* and Kandinsky's *The Yellow Sound*; and *The Archaeology of Sleep.*

Although the run was not a critical success, 8,000 tickets were issued (sold and gratis) during the run at the Joyce. On the opening night of *The Archaeology of Sleep*, in the Gamma III scene, when the Grey Figures in the audience ask an audience member, "Are you afraid if I touch you like this?" Julian, knowing full well what he was doing, touched critic Frank Rich of *The Times* on the inner thigh and asked the question. In his review, which was critical of the dramatic elements of the play, Rich accused Julian of having molested him. Clive Barnes of *The Post* was so amused that he wrote about Rich's discomfort in his review. So the critiques became petty. The critical intelligentsia preferred their Living Theatre downtown; in the Lower East Side, the company would receive many admiring reviews in the future. But the gates to midtown and American high culture would remain closed. We had hoped for gigs in Boston and Philadelphia, but they were not to be. The Joyce engagement closed two weeks early.

Julian had a bit more than another year of life, but what a busy year. Another Hollywood film, *Poltergeist II,* television work, a Samuel Beckett play, *That Time*, which he performd in New York and Germany, and many other activities. His legacy endures and only glows more as the years pass. The critics are forgotten.

ON THE STRUCTURE OF
The Archaeology of Sleep
by Julian Beck

Sleep is not a black hole, a little death that we slip into so that the body at rest can regenerate itself. It is a dual process, one aspect of which is physical regeneration, of course; the other is intense mental activity which influences every moment of our "waking" life.

While sleeping, we go through cycles that are divided into four different phases. During each of these phases, the body undergoes distinct physical changes: change in temperature, pulse, muscle tone, blood pressure, positions, breathing, the eyes move, the body secretes glandular fluids, and the electrical waves emitted by the brain vary.

These waves have specific characteristics according to each of the phases. They are tiny and strongly active during Alpha, the first stage of sleep; slower during Beta, the second stage, when they occasionally burst into strong and rapid pulsations; during Gamma, the waves become slow and more regular, finally reaching their full slowness, regularity, and maximum length in Delta sleep.

We regularly go from one phase to another throughout the night. The cycle repeats four or five times, beginning with a prologue while falling asleep, which corresponds to the Alpha rhythm of the brain. Then we slide into Beta, Gamma, and deep sleep Delta, only to "elevate" ourselves again back into Gamma, Beta, and Alpha.

This time the Alpha phase is underlined by two significant elements. The first involves extremely rapid eye-rolling back and forth. The second is that if the sleeper is awakened at this moment and asked if he/she was dreaming, almost inevitably the answer is affirmative. This teaches us that it is then, during this Alpha phase, that we dream; the dreams in the different Alpha periods within the cycle of a night's sleep correspond to the themes and subjects of the different acts of the same play.

Little is known about what happens during the other phases of sleep. This is why, in the tradition of scientific speculation, one must enter the area of hypotheses. It was recently discovered, however, that when one awakens someone from Delta sleep, asking them, "Were you dreaming?" the person will answer "no"; but if one asks, "What were you thinking about?" they will give some kind of answer. For this reason, Delta sleep has begun to be called "thinking sleep." Beta and Gamma remain more mysterious.

Meditating on the structure of the sleep cycle, thinking of the famous "formulation of dreams" theory hypothesized by Freud, I sensed the glow of a dialectic, which immediately appeared to me as a valid scientific hypothesis and a subject for dramatic study: art as a vehicle for discovery.

The Freudian theory can be roughly articulated thus: a problem arises during the day which elicits memories (related experiences). These memories become subjects of a problem study, which constitutes a dream. The solution to the problem is accomplished through the expression of a wish, and the realization of this wish during the dream cannot exist without a wish-fulfillment being expressed; although the wish always comes up against censorship, which the dream tries to suppress, or to avoid, by discovering the means for its fulfillment.

In addition, I reflected on the assertion of Alfred Adler, a contemporary of Freud, who defines dreams as the mechanism of problem-solving, carried out by "thought"; and that of Herbert Silberez, who supports two functions of the dream, one identifiable with psychoanalysis and the other of a generic nature. Freud strongly opposed these notions, which, according to him, could not admit of scientific justifications. It never occurred to me that he himself, moreover, demonstrated that all the dreams which he so attentively studied and analyzed, with poetry and intelligence, could not conceive of a more philosophical, a more cosmic interpretation.

I decided to probe all of this while creating the text for the play. By putting this material together, I arrived at this formulation. During the Beta phase, the wish is expressed. During Gamma, censorship or restriction is formulated; so that then, in Delta, both the wish and the censorship take the form of "thoughts." The Gamma phase reiterates the censorship factor, then during the second Beta phase there is a recapitulation of the wish. The first Alpha phase of a night becomes the first act, or the presentation of all ideas, materials, conflicts, thoughts, ideas, visions, in the form of a play of high artistic and poetic quality.

When the Alpha phase is exhausted, it is followed by another Beta phase, in which the wish is repeated again; the Gamma and Delta phases reappear, then Gamma and Beta once more until Alpha II is reached; and so on throughout the night, until a lively awakening (when a problem finds a solution, a wish comes true) or a terrifying one due to overwhelmingly powerful censorship, an unrealized wish. It is then that we experience what we call nightmares, or wake disconcerted by the work of sleeping thought, which remains impenetrable and obscure to the waking mind.

The characters of the Sleepers in the play are based on five members of the Living Theatre. Consequently, their dreams abound with images related to The Living Theatre, to themselves and others, to our rehearsals, to our past productions (such as *Prometheus,* which is part of one of Hanon Reznikov's dreams, a character he played), and to our daily life.

Literary and artistic references fill our sleep, its life, and I have carried over many of them through the play's visual and verbal structure. They take the form of homage. Gamma I is inspired by a painting by Ferdinand Hodler, "Die Nacht."

Gamma VI and Beta VI, "War and Peace," are a tribute to Picasso's "Massacre in Korea." Gamma IV, "Brise Marine," consists of verses from a Mallarmé sonnet of the same name. Delta II, "Imagine," is a tribute to John Lennon. The concept of Grey Figures as guardian angels is a tribute to Jean Cocteau. The language of Beta VI is inspired by the Zohar. Alpha I's scenes relating to "The Murder of Gonzago" refer, of course, to *Hamlet*, as a play within a play as well as many other scenes.

Author's remarks from the program of the play at the Maison de la Culture de Nantes. Translated by Ilion Troya from the Frenh translation by Henriette Lüthi.

The Archaeology of Sleep was first performed by The Living Theatre at the Salle Paul Fort in Nantes on June 1, 1983, a co-production of the Maison de la Culture de Nantes and the Ministère de la Culture. It was directed by Judith Malina, with setting, costumes, and lighting by Julian Beck, music by Raaja Fischer, translation into French by Henriette Lüthi.

Cast of Characters

THE SLEEPERS

ANTONIA	Antonia Matera
CATHÉRINE	Cathérine Marchand
HANON	Hanon Reznikov
CHRISTIAN	Christian Vollmer
TOM	Tom Walker

———

THE GREY FIGURES

SABUHL	Ilion Troya
DIVINE	Rain House
RABBI KRAZY KAT	Stephan Schulberg
DANDELION	Horacio Palacios
PANDORA	Henriette Lüthi
LIZA	Maria Nora
THE DOCTOR	Dirk Szuszies
SHE	Helga Jeske
AMUH	Mina Lande

———

THE CITY OF NANTES   Isha Manna Beck

NOTE: The role of The City of Nantes, when the play is played in Paris or New York or wherever, becomes The City of Paris or The City of New York or The City of Wherever, as the case may be.

185

The Setting

A black stage containing five grey beds. Across the back of the stage: the tracks of a Train of Thought.

The Grey Figures

Each Sleeper in this play surely has one in particular. Who are they? The soul, the mind, the spirit, the heart, the alter-ego, the eros, the double, the true self, the false self, the imagined Other, our schizophrenia, and our multiplicity. In the end there's little telling who is who.

THE ARCHAEOLOGY OF SLEEP

THE GATES OF ALPHA

SCENE I
THE SECRET

The Temple of the Cats.

Light filters into the temple, and the great temple creatures representing *kamrisch, la béatitude du monde animal*, steal in silently and take their places in two long files facing each other across the front of the stage.

They bask in the tenebrous light, motionless, solemn, like statues of themselves.

They have, in fact, arranged themselves to suit the splendor of their world.

They are each magnificent in their degree of awareness of the unique significance of one another,

They chant in unison the fabled tribal *Miaou*, which reverberates like the twanging of enormous harps.

Simultaneously they ceremonially perform an étude; one thinks of the precision of the tea ceremony, an étude defining the divine nature of the cat.

The étude is also performed by the cats to hypnotize visitors to the temple.

Scene 2
The Stranger

A Stranger, wearing a bowler hat, a suit and tie, a raincoat, emerges from the audience and enters the temple.

The Stranger salutes two of the cats.

The Stranger attracts the cats with glittering collars of light in which he attires them.

The two cats respond with trust.

The other cats scamper stealthily away.

The Stranger then leads the two cats by the leash to the Train of Thought.

A cage arrives on the Train of Thought, moving from stage left toward stage right. The cage stops like a train at a station.

The Stranger leads the two cats into the cage, closes the cage, picks up the carriage chain, slings it over his shoulder, and, with great labor, pulls the cage off toward stage left.

The cage pulls in its wake a white satin divan on which a young woman sleeps.

The Stranger disappears stage left; but the cage with the cats and the couch with the sleeping woman remain in view on the now motionless Train of Thought.

The Gates of Alpha

Scene 3
The Alpha Cantata: Beauty Sleep

On the Train of Thought: the figure of the sleeping woman in·a basin of golden light, and the two cats in the cage, their collars glowing in the dim light.

Five SLEEPERS in a cloud of GREY FIGURES float onto the stage.

As the cloud passes each of the five beds, one of .the SLEEPERS ritually drifts from the group and prepares ceremonially to go to ˈsleep. When the cloud has crossed the stage ˈall of the five SLEEPERS are falling asleep and the cloud of GREY FIGURES drifts over the edge of the stage and up the aisle toward the rear of the theatre. All the while the Grey Figures are chanting.

SEMI-CHORUS I (*slow, extenuated*): Beauty-sleep.....

SEMI-CHORUS II (*low, rapid*): Slumber deep-sleep sound-sleep heavy-sleep troubled-sleep sleep of the just.....

SEMI-CHORUS I: Arms of Morpheus.....

SEMI-CHORUS II: Hypnos Sandman half-sleep drowse first-sleep light-sleep cat-nap nap.....

SEMI-CHORUS I: La Sonnambula.....

SEMI-CHORUS II: Soporific night-cap sleeping pill sedative barbiturate sleeping-draught.....

SEMI-CHORUS I: Sleeping Beauty.....

SEMI-CHORUS II: Opiate poppy mandragora opium morphine sleeping dog.....

SEMI-CHORUS I: Lotus eater.....

SEMI-CHORUS II: Rest restfulness comatose lullaby lazy go to bed.....

SEMI-CHORUS I: Encephalitis lethargica.....

The Gates of Alpha

Scene 4
The Lantern Slides of Day Residue

As the cloud of Grey Figures moves up the aisle of the theatre continuing to chant the Alpha Cantata, a spotlight shines on each bed—one at a time, one after the other—for a precise number of seconds, the number of seconds diminishing mathematically as the scene progresses.

Bed 1:	Bed 2:	Bed 3:	Bed 4:	Bed 5:
7 secs.	7 secs.	7 secs.	7 secs.	7 secs.
6 "	6 "	6 "	6 "	6 "
5 "	5 "	5 "	5 "	5 "
4 "	4 "	4 "	4 "	4 "
3 "	3 "	3 "	3 "	3 "

As the lights snap on and off, one of the Grey Figures (Ilion) calls out over the chorus:

Grey Figure (Ilion): Which one was saved, only one of a thousand single grapes?

Antonia (*mumbling in her Alpha state*): Liquid crystal, nuts and bolts.

Grey Figure (Ilion): What memory was that of Spain, where olives swallowed testicles?

Tom: Good food, an afternoon.

Grey Figure (Ilion): What bus of dead revealed the Koran's honey date?

Cathérine: Not mine, too soon.

GREY FIGURE (ILION): Who lost a mother, ravaged truth, a New York tiger?

CHRISTIAN: A kind of tooth, a mirror.

GREY FIGURE (ILION): What kind of splendid sentence soaked with bitter water tasted sweet?

HANON: Talmud lustre, talcum white.

Blackout.

The Gates of Alpha

Scene 5
The Myoclonic Jerk

Sudden interruption. Harsh light on the cage on the Train of Thought.

THE STRANGER, now a white-coated doctor, is giving one of the cats an injection with a hypodermic needle in the back of the neck. The cat spasms three times and falls. Loud sound.

THE SLEEPERS spasm thrice.

Blackout.

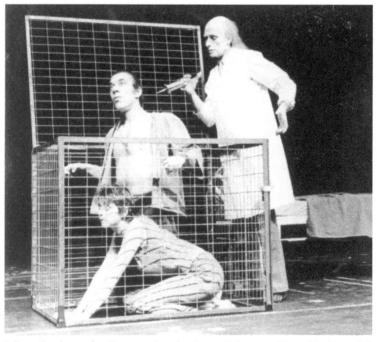

Julian Beck as the Doctor (at the Joyce Theater, New York), with Stephan Schulberg and Maria Nora

192

THE GATES OF ALPHA

SCENE 6
STRUCK BLIND LIKE THE SODOMITES

In the darkness, the sound of the tapping of canes. Everyone has been struck blind. Wearing dark glasses and carrying white canes, the GREY FIGURES begin to make their way from the back of the theatre toward the stage space.

At the same time, a blind man carrying a large Braille book hesitatingly makes his way forward from the rear of the stage. As the BLIND MAN (ILION) passes one of the SLEEPERS (HANON), he hold the book out to him. HANON runs his fingers over the page and reads in his sleep.

SLEEPER (HANON): "Each eye in blinded slumber summer closes...."

As the BLIND MAN with the book of Braille leaves him, he meets the other blind people now moving across the stage. He extends the book to them and two of them pause to read.

FIRST BLIND FIGURE (RAIN): "Destitute of the sense of light..."

The cluster moves on a little and then the second blind person pauses to read.

SECOND BLIND FIGURE (HELGA): "To the bodily eye, self is a perpetual blinder..."

THE BLIND ONE with the book of Braille descends into the audience space, extends the book to an audience member, and instructs them.

THE BLIND ONE WITH THE BOOK OF BRAILLE (ILION): Would you like to read Braille? Take the book. Use both hands, one beside the other. Hardly touch the paper. The right hand guides, the index finger of the left reads... (*He reads aloud as the spectator traces hisher fingers over the letters*): "The...

blinding...of...passion...putting...night...in...the...
eyes..." Hmmmmmmmmmm... (*He goes on.*) The fingers
must glide across the page in a straight line. Yes. "The...
darkness...which...lay...blindingly...on...the...hearts...
and...souls...of...humankind." Hmmmmmmmmmm...(*He
begins to move back onto the stage space reciting from memory
a final phrase as he disappears in the dark.*) "The darkness
of his mind obscured everything his eyes beheld..."
Hmmmmmmmmmmm...

Blackout.

BETA-I

THE INTERNATIONAL FESTIVAL OF POETRY

Sound of Beta Wave: a powerful drone with occasional spindles. The GREY FIGURES enter like a crowd of spectators coming into an auditorium where a poetry reading is about to take place. They seat themselves on the floor facing the SLEEPERS. One of the GREY FIGURES goes excitedly from bed to bed waking the SLEEPERS and announcing the Festival, at the same time distributing pieces of paper—the texts of the poems to be read—to each of the SLEEPERS.

GREY FIGURE (RAIN): Amsterdam Poetry Festival— You sit up straight—o you sad rabbis—move your jaws—Amsterdam Poetry Festival!

One after the other, the SLEEPERS sit on the edge of their beds and read.

HANON:

I would   hold   out   this cup   to you

AKIBA PEOPLE:

I would bend this   dark   fender   back:
    Pour   even   a pitcher   of darkness
    into   a   glass of   light
    and   the   wine
    still   glows

TOM:

Listen   dark   angel
    black poet   I   implore   god
    in the temple   of your   body
    five   times   free
ten times   free

CATHÉRINE:

au premier feu
il   fractura   le loquet
au deuxième feu
il   rompit   la chaine
au troisième feu
il   ouvrit   la porte
au quatrième feu
il   découpe   l'air
au cinquième feu
il   rencontra   son coeur

ANTONIA:

luna   di raccolta
luna   di semina
luna   di maturità
luna   di giusta misura
luna   di frutti d'estate

CHRISTIAN:

Er wurde zornig   und   schrie
ich   bin   in einem Schildwachters linder
ich   bin   in einem   senkrechten   Sarg
ich   bin in einem Stück   Staats Eigentum
ich werde   den Wunsch   nicht wiederstehen
es   zu   beenden

Applause, like a wave rolling up on a beach and out. All of
the SLEEPERS have returned to sleep.
Blackout.
In the blackout, the sleeping CITY OF NANTES slides out of
view.

GAMMA-I

DIE NACHT

Sound change. Another wavelength.

Lights grow very dim. Gamma light.

Moving very slowly, the GREY FIGURES rise and cover the SLEEPERS ceremonially with huge lengths of black cloth. They slide into bed with the SLEEPERS or, covering themselves also, lie stretched out about the floor. Only the heads and the flesh of a few arms and legs are visible.

The GREY FIGURE .(HENRIETTE) in bed with CHRISTIAN, shrouded in black, rises to a crouch at the foot of his bed. CHRISTIAN opens his eyes, leaning on his elbows rises aghast and gazes at the shrouded figure with pale horror. A few low incomprehensible sounds of fright emerge from his throat, the sound of powerlessness and fear.

Homage to Ferdinand Hodler.

Blackout.

Delta-I

Thinking Sleep

In the blackout, the heavy sound of Deep Sleep: a low murmuring of voices all speaking at once.

In the blackout, the City of Nantes, fast asleep, in a lighted glass box, slides into view.

The Grey Figures and the Sleepers lie beside one another whispering, kissing, murmuring, caressing, breathing heavily, softly stretching, sometimes simply basking in the warmth of the affection of friendship. All the time talking.

Two of the Grey Figures slip into the audience space.

The cycle of audible dialogue:

Antonia: What then is possible for me?

Grey Figure (Rain): To select the helmsman, the sailors, the day, the moment.

Grey Figure (Dirk) (*in the audience space, addressing a spectator*): What can I do when death appears as an evil? (*Supplying the answer*): You have to have an argument all prepared, that it's our duty to avoid evil, and that this duty is a pleasure.

Cathérine: When you're consciously awake does the world remain steadily the same to your eyes and ears?

Grey Figure (Horacio): I can pierce it with rays from our illuminating focus of attention—with varying success.

Grey Figure (Maria Nora) (*in the audience space, addressing a spectator*): What can a fortune teller see that is of greater importance than danger, illness, death? (*Supplying the answer*): To learn to tell the signs that are the characteristics of good and bad.

Hanon: For instance, it's within the power of the human mind to count thousands or millions multiplied without

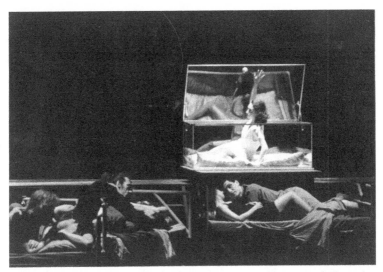

Isha Manna Beck as The City of Sleep arrives on the Train of Thought; foreground, Sleepers and Grey Figures including Stephan Schulberg and Horacio Palacio

end, but can such a number ever become reality?

GREY FIGURE (STEPHAN): What becomes actual can be counted as One.

GREY FIGURE (DIRK) (*addressing a spectator*): The natural world, is it there always for you, or does it sometimes drift into ordered arithmetics and become alien? (*Supplying the answer*): I see them differently sometimes, yes, but when I don't think about it, they are always there before me, one and the same.

CHRISTIAN: Where am I to look for the good and the evil?

GREY FIGURE (HENRIETTE): Externals aren't under my control; moral choice, however, that's something else.

TOM: I am aware of a world endlessly spread out in space, spread out in time, becoming and also already become, and without end. No ring surrounds it, it never exhausts itself…

GREY FIGURE (ILION): What you and I actually perceive

is both pervaded and girded with a depth only dimly apprehended...

GREY FIGURE (DIRK) (*addressing a spectator*): It's necessary to develop the power to tell the true from the false. That's clear, no? (*Supplying the answer*): Ah, that's another kind of power...

Suddenly the CITY OF NANTES opens the lid of the glass box in which she's been sleeping and sits upright. She is about to sleep-walk. She rises and steps unerringly out of the box. Her eyelids seem almost closed. She moves cautiously and never bumps into anything. She moves in one direction, then changes where she is going, as if she were correcting an error.

A GREY FIGURE: Shhhhhhh!

Everyone stops and stares. The SLEEPERS and the other GREY FIGURES watch intently.

Two women, GREY FIGURES, on the side of the stage space, huddled together, like two old Irish women, crones, awed, follow her action, and comment on it.

FIRST GREY WOMAN (MINA): Every night!

SECOND GREY WOMAN (HELGA): She's doing it again...

FIRST GREY WOMAN (MINA): Look how her eyes are closed but she is never going to fall or stumble... Oh, she's beginning to moan again...

SECOND GREY WOMAN (HELGA): She's looking for something...

FIRST GREY WOMAN (MINA): No, she's looking for someone...

THE CITY OF NANTES pokes around in one of the beds and gets desperate when she doesn't find what she's looking for. Suddenly she pulls out the Nantes telephone directory from under one of the mattresses.

THE CITY OF NANTES: Serge Dréanon, 40, rue Claude Lorrain, 20.58.08; Emile Drouet, 1, rue Luxembourg, 47.55.25;

Elisabeth Dubois, 20, rue Paul Bellamy, 43.10.63, Ah.....
no, no, no, no,no,no,no,no, no answer. It rings and rings
and rings. Never any answer. *(She stops in front of one of the*
Sleepers, *lifts the cover from her face)*: Maybe dead?... *(A cat
miaous. She goes to her, puts her arms around her, and strokes her
affectionately.)* Ah, Liza..... To be, to bed, to bed, to bed, to
bed...

She and the cat—Maria Nora—move toward the Train
of Thought. She reenters her box, closes the lid. The cat leaps
up and stares at her like a guardian in a Goya.

The Grey Figures and the Sleepers return to sleep.

The City of Nantes and the cat begin to slide out of view.
Dimdown. Blackout.

GAMMA-II

THE SLEEP LABORATORY

Very dim light.

The SLEEPERS and the GREY FIGURES stretch in sleep movements appropriate to the Gamma phase of sleep.

The low drone of whispers heard in Delta-I changes to the more rolling waves of Gamma which become in the course of the scene more and more the beautiful purring of cats.

The DOCTOR enters in white jacket. He is followed by three assistants, also white-jacketed, who appear rolling in on the Train of Thought. At the same time a small control table comes in from the other direction on the Train of Thought. There are many electrodes attached to it.

While the DOCTOR speaks, the aides attach the electrodes to the SLEEPERS and the GREY FIGURES in the beds. The DOCTOR stands in bright light down center. The aides work by means of pencil flashlights; what they are doing remains relatively indistinct.

The DOCTOR speaks in the manner of the professor, secure, opinionated, condescending to his listeners. He has a German accent.

THE DOCTOR: Sleep research, as you all know, is an infant, a mere infant, among the sciences. It only began thirty years ago in Chicago. Very important. They noticed for the first time in history—can you imagine how stupid and unobservant we are!—that when you wake someone from Paradoxical Sleep and ask,"Were you dreaming?" they almost inevitably say "Yes."

Paradoxical Sleep. Does anyone here know what it is? Good. I tell you. If you take the trouble to use your eyes at this late moment in history—you will notice that the eyes of the sleeper—under closed lids naturally—are sometimes moving back and forth. And whenever that happens the subject is surely dreaming. Yes, the subject is surely dreaming.

And this is only one of four distinct kinds of sleep. We pass through four phases every night. They constitute a cycle. Each cycle lasts about an hour and forty-five minutes. And we each go through four or five cycles every night.

Now, we can—without causing any discomfort—attach electrodes, as we are doing now in the laboratory—to the scalps of the subjects. A little jelly and salt will hold this little piece of metal on the subject's head all night; and we can see his electroencephalograph, we can measure his heartbeat, und so weiter. The electroencephalograph is a way of measuring the tiny electrical waves emitted by the brain. They go like this: zhzhzhzhzhzhzhzhzhzhzhzhzhzhzhzh… (*He demonstrates with his finger.*) A small spindly irregular rapid rhythm—Alpha rhythm. In this Alpha phase the eyes move rapidly, darting back and forth, as if watching a film with quickly changing images. You understand? Alpha rhythm. This rhythm occurs as we fall asleep and more pronouncedly when we dream.

Then there is a Beta rhythm, and a Gamma rhythm and a Delta. Alpha Beta Gamma Delta. All this we can learn just by looking at ourselves asleep. We just woke up to this.

BUT IT IS NOT ENOUGH. Not enough to solve the millennia-old mystery of sleep. For fuller understanding of this secret secret knowledge, science fortunately can go beyond superficial observation. But systematic experiments are necessary. (*The* SLEEPERS *and the* GREY FIGURES *begin to transform into cats. They first assume the majestic positions of temple cats. Then they begin to curl up and go to sleep and to follow the phases of sleep, illustrating the* DOCTOR's *talk.*) Obviously such experiments cannot always be performed on man; so it is necessary to use animals. (*Faint laboratory lights on* SLEEPER-CATS.)

The cat, like the human being, passes into Paradoxical Sleep. At this time the cat's body is altogether relaxed.

Here you see a group of cats all in Delta or Deep Sleep. Sometimes we call this Thinking Sleep. Now you will see the cats pass through Gamma and Beta phases and enter REM or Alpha Sleep. See how they stretch and shift. Now see the neck muscles slump. Ja! And the eyes are rapidly moving. Ja, ja.

But what is really happening? Physiologically? For this we must go inside— (*The aides are moving among the cats, holding them down, making surgical marks and cuts on the cats' heads.*)

The presence of two distinct alternating kinds of sleep, clearly analogous to what is seen in the human, means that experiments on cat paradoxical sleep are relevant to human sleep.

On this group of cats we make cuts through the brainstem—separating the lower part wholly from the upper—you know the brain has two parts, just like the Nile. With this group of cats we are removing the upper brain completely, including tbe cerebral cortex. What might be called a rear-brained animal is being created. It still goes through the different phases of sleep so far as can be judged by the cats' muscle tone and tension. But can an animal with only half a brain dream? So it appears, but what does this mean?

So, when they relax—as in Alpha or Paradoxical Sleep— we give them an electrical buzz— (*Loud buzz*)—and they seem to wake for a few seconds. Then as soon as they relax again we give them another shock. (*Loud buzz*) This is the same experiment— (*Buzz. Each time there is a buzz the animals start and wake and then fall back to Paradoxical Sleep positions.*)— we have performed on—(*Buzz*)—on normal human beings—(*Buzz*)—But how can you—(*Buzz*)—how can you—(*Buzz*)—deprive—(*Buzz*)—an animal with only-

(*Buzz. Buzz.*)—half a brain—(*Buzz*)—from dreaming?—(*Buzz*)—Huh?—(*Buzz*)—How? How? (*The animals keep twitching incessantly.*) Only a physiological explanation is possible… Is the need to dream psychological…or is it physiological? Huh? Huh? Huh?

Buzz. Buzz. Buzz. Twitch. Twitch. Twitch.
Lights fade to black.

Beta-II

The Sammy Rosenstock Memorial Synagogue

The sound of prayer. A synagogue of people davening. Light reveals people covered with white prayer shawls, mumbling in ancient language, moving rhythmically back and forth.

A Dada Readymade—a miniature ark containing a scroll—appears on the Train of Thought.

In a circle of light, downstage center, a Sleeper (Hanon) is slowly wrestling with the Doctor. They roll on the ground.

Out of the sound of prayer occasional words become clear, emerging from individual voices, all male:

prayer sound   SAMMY ROSENSTOCK   prayer sound
DADA IS A WAY OF LIFE   prayer sound   DADA
MEANS NOTHING   prayer sound   prayer sound
prayer sound

The scroll is brought to the center bed on which a reader's desk rests. A reader (Stephan) reads; occasional words float out over the sound of the collective beta-prayer-wave rhythm.

The Reader (Stephan): And Jaakov was left alone (*prayer sound*) alone (*prayer sound*) and there wrestled (*prayer sound*) with a man until day broke (*prayer sound*) and the hollow of his thigh (*prayer sound*) put out of joint (*prayer sound*) what is your name (*prayer sound*) what is your name (*prayer sound*) what is your.....

His voice fades. The lights fade. Blackout.

ALPHA-I
(PARADOXICAL SLEEP—REM SLEEP—D-STATE)

"ACT I"
THE EXPOSITION

Order of the Dreams

1. Terry and the Pirates (CATHÉRINE's dream)
2. The Way of the World (TOM's dream)
3. A Christian Becomes a Wolf (CHRISTIAN's dream)
4. Mata Hari's Secret (CATHÉRINE's dream)
5. The Chase (HANON's dream)
6. The Waves (CATHÉRINE's dream)
7. The Murder of Gonzago (1) (HANON's dream)
8. Antonia's Immobility (ANTONIA's dream)
9. Losing Time (TOM's dream)
10. The Emerging Species (CATHÉRINE's dream)
11. The Acting Lesson (1) (CHRISTIAN's dream)
12. In the Mosque (TOM's dream)
13. The Acting Lesson (2) (CHRISTIAN's dream, or ANTONIA's)
14. The Murder of Gonzago (2) (HANON's dream)
15. Muzzein Time (TOM and CATHÉRINE's joint dream)
16. The Juggernaut (ANTONIA's Dream)
17. The Bathing Beauty Becomes a Buddha (CATHÉRINE's dream)
18. The Murder of Gonzago (3) (HANON's dream)

Note:
The chorus is a dream mass.

It creates the architecture for each scene, the geography, the epoch.

They are a moving mass of unconscious sources out of which emerge lost ideas, memories, and preoccupations.

The dreams fold and flow in and out of each other, GREY
FIGURES moving amorphously in and out of frame and focus.
Blackouts slice one dreamer's dream from another's.
Each scene has a variant rapid eye movement rhythm.
The scenes are played rapidly and very rapidly.

Alpha-I
Scene 1

Terry and the Pirates
(Cathérine's Dream)

The City of Nantes, asleep on her divan, slides in on the Train of Thought.

Grey Figures engulf Cathérine. Carry her off. She falls. She implores. She lies under them. They raise her over their heads. She appears to fly. They lower her under them and stand like sea-ferns undulating over her.

Cathérine:
Fish flew from the ocean to paralyse me.
I fell before them.
Under their feet I could evade being questioned.

Chorus:
Because I knew I didn't have my passport.

Cathérine:
They raised me over their heads.
I grew to the size of a dirigible.

Chorus:
That was the First Deception.

Cathérine:
An anchor, I lay on the ocean floor
looking at sea anemones.

Blackout.

Alpha-I
Scene 2

The Way of the World
(Tom's Dream)

The GREY FIGURE OF ILION bends over the SLEEPER, TOM, and wakes him with a kiss. TOM rises. TOM follows. They move, one behind the other: Sabu leading the blind Thief of Baghdad through the streets of escape.

TOM:
   He appeared fully clothed.
   I could see him though I was blind.
   He was really naked.
   I thought it a clever way to avoid detection.
   He couldn't have been a policeman because he was naked.
   But only I knew this.

   Blackout.

Alpha-I
Scene 3

A Christian Becomes a Wolf
(Christian's Dream)

CHRISTIAN falls from his bed with a wolfish howl, rolls on the floor in a kind of agony of protest at what is happening to him. He is transforming.

CATHÉRINE: Christian!

CHRISTIAN tries to answer but cannot. Muffled sounds.

ANTONIA (*from her bed*): Christian, what time is the moon?

More anguished attempts to speak. Suddenly a clear and terrible howl. He is now a wolf, he has the teeth of a wolf, he prowls.

The DOCTOR appears. He wears a light-reflector strap around his head and carries a cross.

THE DOCTOR: Christian!

The WOLF laughs.

The WOLF bounds about.

The WOLF's face becomes covered with blood after tearing at the shadow imprinted on TOM's empty bed. Snips of chewed cloth hang from his mouth.

The WOLF leaps up onto the Train of Thought and menaces the sleeping CITY OF NANTES.

CATHÉRINE: Christian!

The WOLF weeps.

THE DOCTOR: Komm her!

The CHRISTIAN WOLF returns to bed exhausted. Blackout.

Alpha-I
Scene 4

Mata Hari's Secret
(Cathérine's Dream)

Cathérine suddenly springs up from the bottom of the ocean where she has been lying. She swings a big man to the ground. They speak unintelligibly. She pins him to the ground. She overcomes him.

Cathérine:
I can't be changed!
I can't be changed from a woman into a man!

They speak unintelligibly.
Blackout.

Alpha-I
Scene 5

The Chase
(Hanon's Dream)

Hanon moves in sudden stops and starts, scurrying from bed to bed, moving like a criminal, hiding behind and under the beds.

Doctor's Voice: Komm her!

Hanon:
Lechem oo-mayim haym tovim m'od. (Bread and water are very good.)

Doctor's Voice: Komm her!

Hanon:
The rule of the game
must be
that you must either move
keep moving or talk.

Doctor's Voice: Komm her!

Hanon:
If you stop
then the poison comes in
either on the absent sound waves—
THE SILENCE!

The Doctor: Komm her!

Hanon (*breathless*):
If I can get home
I can find my old notes—

The City of Nantes (*tenderly, in her sleep*): Komm her...

Hanon flies into bed. Blackout.

Alpha-I
Scene 6

The Waves
(Cathérine's Dream)

A woman, Cathérine, lies atop four Grey Figures. She is swimming on top of the waves.

Cathérine: My arm's a propellor.

Chorus of Waves:
Only the waves already knew
that terrible messages
were concealed inside the fish by now.

Blackout.

Alpha-I
Scene 7

The Murder of Gonzago (1)
(Hanon's Dream)

The Figure in Flight, Hanon, leaps onto a bed. It becomes a boat. A crew of Grey Figures rowing.

Hanon:
> Full sail ahead!
> The Destination calls us!
> We are going to discover new lands!

Chorus:
> His eyes are rolling like dice.
> He's playing with chance.
> Look in the rear-view mirror!

Hanon:
> The coral reef!

The boat hits the Doctor, it passes on top of him as if he were the reef. It grates to a stop. The Chorus leaps out of the bed-boat and tilts it upwards so that it stands on its nose. Hanon lies flat against it as if it were a raft.

The City of Nantes sits bolt upright, legs crossed, like a fortune-teller, gazing into a round stone which she holds before her like a crystal ball. She rises and moves toward Hanon, eyes fixed on the stone which she continues to hold before her.

Hanon:
> If I keep my eyes rolling
> the Doctor will be paralysed.

The City of Nantes (*prophetic voice*): Let the wind blow out of your eyes.

She walks forward and places the stone in his hand. He gazes into it as if it were Yorick's skull, but remains still flattened against the boat.

CHORUS: Immobile like a stone in the Place Royale.

HANON: Point you out of Egypt.

THE CITY OF NANTES (*curling up on the floor at* HANON'S *feet and going back to sleep*): Tst. Tst. Curare. The venom of an Amazon snake.

HANON (*contemplating the stone*):
Rehearse. Rehearse.
The only defense that carries any weight.

Blackout.

Alpha-I
Scene 8

Antonia's Immobility
(Antonia's Dream)

Everyone asleep. In the back, on the Train of Thought, the CITY OF NANTES again curled up on her couch in a cloud of yellow light, asleep.

TOM (*calling out in his sleep as if over a canyon*): Antonia!

ANTONIA (*turning over in bed*): Nmmmmmm.

Tom: Antonia!

Antonia: When's the rehearsal? Already?

She turns over and goes back to sleep. The CHRISTIAN-WOLF pads over and leaps up on her bed and looks at her as she sleeps. Low wolf howl.

Blackout.

Alpha-I
Scene 9

Losing Time
(Tom's Dream)

Tom and the Grey Figure Ilion moving like criminals through the forest of people.

Tom (*conspiratorial tone*): The rehearsal is at two, isn't it?

Grey Figure (Ilion) (*taking him by the hand, they scurry to another alley*): There is no time here.

Chorus:
Tom sweats.
His pores like vats of steam.

Blackout.

Alpha-I
Scene 10

The Emerging Species
(Cathérine's Dream)

Cathérine pulls herself out of the ocean and struggles to her feet on the sand of the beach. She shakes the seaweed from her hair and looks out over the island. In the background, the City of Nantes lies asleep on her divan.

Cathérine: Washed up on the beach like Venus. (*She looks out over the audience.*) Deserted. No one. Nothing. Wild. A jungle!

Chorus (*in the background, a South Sea air*):
Wai alai alou alou
Wai alai alou alou aloooom
Wai waia waia waialoomah

Cathérine (*calling out over the audience space*): Allo-o-o-o-o-o-o-o-o-o-o (*No answer. She walks timidly further onto the forestage.*) Allo-o-o-o-o-o-o-o-o-o-o-o

The City of Nantes (*asleep, but sitting up and waving*): Allo-o-o-o-o-o-o-o-o-o-o-o

Blackout.

ALPHA-I
SCENE 11

THE ACTING LESSON (1)
(CHRISTIAN'S DREAM)

CHRISTIAN, crouched on ANTONIA's bed, snarls like a wolf.

ANTONIA (*waking, horrified*): Wolf!

CHRISTIAN (*reprovingly*): Antonia!

CHORUS:
   Played a wolf
   in a children's play
   and never came back!

ANTONIA (*gripping him with intensity*):
   Since you are an actor
   you should be able to effect
   an autotransformation!

CHRISTIAN (*with great effort he speaks*): I will play Ekdal.

ANTONIA: You must be very strong, Eilert.

CHRISTIAN: I'm crying!

ANTONIA (*in disgust*): Ugh! Not like a baby!

CHORUS: Telegram!

CHRISTIAN: Urgent!

   Blackout.

The Mosque
(Tom's Dream)

The Chorus bows to the ground, facing east. Dancing before him seductively, Tom's Grey Figure guide, Sabuhl (Ilion), leads him into the mosque.

Tom (*taking* Sabuhl's *arm*):
But I can't come in here, with my European hair.
I won't know what to do. What if I'm discovered?

Sabuhl:
Just bow to the ground and pray...
Prayer is a universe...

Tom: But I don't know the words...

Sabuhl: What are words? Turn your heart strings into a lute.
Play.

Tom bows to the ground. Sabuhl bows on top of him. They move up and down. Image: sodomy.
Blackout.

Alpha-I
Scene 13

The Acting Lesson (2)
(Christian's Dream, or Antonia's)

CHRISTIAN (*executing an étude that requires great strain*):
Watch closely. Use your eyes.
When the hair will fall from my body.
It is called the Lyre.
Do it with me this time.
When the exercise passes the zenith
Our bodies will begin to sing.

ANTONIA: Ah, this I can't do. I love it. (ANTONIA *and several* GREY FIGURES *join the workshop.* STEPHAN *comes and whispers something to* CHRISTIAN.) Isha, you should practice this too.

The CITY OF NANTES wakes, and, eagerly leaping from her couch, comes and joins the workshop.

CHRISTIAN (*he begins to make sounds*):
Hya eeeya hee
hya eeeya hee   allabba   ba   mmmmeneea
habbbbb   llmmanaa

The students join in the sounds. The bodies burst into music.
Blackout.

Alpha-I
Scene 14

The Murder of Gonzago (2)
(Hanon's Dream)

HANON is still pinned to the boat-raft-bed, meditating on the stone. STEPHAN, a GREY FIGURE, stands beside him, a shadow, also meditating on a stone.

GREY FIGURE (STEPHAN) (*leaping forward and placing his head on the stone*): Eureka! The stone's a pillow!

THE DOCTOR (*pinning* HANON *to the bed, while* HANON *struggles to leave*): You can't leave now!

HANON: I have to go to rehearsal.

THE DOCTOR (*crumpling into sleep*): Rehearsal...means... nothing...

HANON (*he moves like a sleep-walker*): So I shall show you the murder of Gonzago... The play's the thing wherein I'll catch the conscience of— (*He notices the Grey Figure of* STEPHAN.) —You are...?

GREY FIGURE (STEPHAN): The king...

Blackout.

Alpha-I
Scene 15

Muezzin Time
(Tom and Cathérine's Joint Dream)

The sound of the call of a muezzin. Everyone curves to the ground and up again, like palms being bent back and forth by an invisible force. Tom begins to spasm and contort instead of swaying.

Cathérine (*stealthily entering the prayer zone*): Fantômas!

Tom is struggling with the Grey Figure of Sabuhl (Ilion) who is trying to help him execute the bow correctly while other Muslims (Chorus) look at Tom critically. Cathérine now penetrates the mosque itself and speaks furtively to Tom.

Chorus: A woman is entering the mosque! Ay yai yai!

Cathérine: Don't believe. Don't bow to anyone. You are not a carpet. Danger lies everywhere. Even in all this beauty.

Chorus: Like carpets.

Cathérine: Spies. Spies. It isn't sunset yet and the muezzin is already losing time.

The sound of the muezzin grows louder and louder.

Tom (*rising up*): Spies! SPIES!

Blackout.

ALPHA-I
SCENE 16

THE JUGGERNAUT
(ANTONIA'S DREAM)

A temple of reclining Buddhas. ANTONIA moves among them scrubbing the floor.

CHORUS: Buddhas bless. Buddhas crush.

A Buddha begins to roll forward and rolls right over ANTONIA leaving her squashed on the ground.

ANTONIA: I thought to myself, how am I to interpret this?

She lies on the ground twitching.
Blackout.

Alpha-I
Scene 17

The Bathing Beauty
(Cathérine's Dream)

Cathérine (*walking among the debris on the shore*): I must get off this island.

Chorus: Isolated.

The City of Nantes, dressed as a bathing beauty, appears on the Train of Thought, a diagonal stripe, "Miss Nantes," across her torso.

Cathérine (*picking up arms and legs, looking at the bodies*):
Driftwood. Shell oil drums.
No survivors.
Horacio!

The Grey Figure of Horacio (Cathérine *has raised up his arm but it doen't move*):
La mujer que viene
una oliva negra tiene.

The City of Nantes struts forward, weaving her way among the debris.

Chorus:
Beauty hurts. Beauty takes. Beauty decays.
Beauty drugs. Beauty fades. Beauty departs.

The City of Nantes:
Beauty weeps.

She collapses weeping on Hanon's bed-raft-boat, which is standing up at right angles to the floor.

Cathérine stoops and embraces Horacio, touches him, strokes him, but he does not respond.

CATHÉRINE:
    Turned to stone
    out of…
    STAGE FRIGHT.

    Blackout.

Alpha-I
Scene 18

The Murder of Gonzago (3)
(Hanon's Dream)

Hanon (*jumping into the audience space*): Please, can we all take places, please! The Murder of Gonzago. We're losing time. Now, I pray you, trippingly on the tongue. For purposes of the rehearsal, out here, in the audience space, is the court. Set up the stage. Stephan, you should take your place somewhere out here. Antonia! Where is she?

Antonia (*offstage*): I'm getting the crowns.

Hanon: Isha, can you get into the Player Queen costume. Julian, would you stand in for the Player King now. (Ilion *and* Isha *appear in Player King and Queen costumes.*) Julian, go ahead.

The Grey Figure of Ilion (*as Player King*): Biyok, strommm, esp. Pah.

Hanon: No, more precise: Biyokkk. Strom, esp. PAH!

Ilion: Biyok, strom, esp. PAH!

Isha (*as Player Queen*): Maa goon.

Hanon (*nervously, from the house*): Again. My god, please, it is late.

Cathérine (*rising in her bed*): It is late! (*She falls back to sleep.*)

Hanon: Stephan and Antonia, go ahead.

Stephan and Antonia from the house, a duet.

Stephan: Ezz braaat naaaa'at t'aat.

Antonia: Baia Baia…

Stephan: Dzeep. Aaaaaaaazzzzzzaaaaazzz

ANTONIA: N'iv, niv dzot tuhn—

HANON: Listen to me: dzot tuhn... But let's skip to when the king lies down to go to sleep. (ILION *lies down.*) No, the line's not good. Like this. (*He shows him how to recline like a Buddha.*) But with each movement, a vocal hieroglyph, like this: Pizee, Oz, Wip, Ah! Ying! (*He goes to* CHRISTIAN's *bed, who lies there sleeping, jerks him out of the bed, steers him toward the little inner stage.*) Now, Christian, you must come on like a revolutionary, moving with Tarquin's ravishing strides, and pour the leprous distillment in his ear.

CHRISTIAN: BBB. MMM. RRR. SbbbbRRRbb. (*He places his index finger in* ILION's *ear.* ISHA, *the Player Queen, screams.*)

STEPHAN: Alarum!

The whole court screams like cats. The performers move like cats, wild, through the audience, screaming, they swarm around the stage space.

STEPHAN:
Torches! Torches!
Wahrp! Bradneesh! Miaouuu......

Pandemonium. The SLEEPERS throw themselves into their beds. The GREY FIGURES take cat positions guarding the beds. The screaming fades quickly to a soft purring sound. The SLEEPERS are in their beds.

Dim down and out.

Beta-III

One Is One

Whirring Beta rhythm.

Asleep in the arms of a Grey Figure, the City of Nantes appears on the Train of Thought. It is very dark. She raises her arms in a gesture of supplication.

The City of Nantes: Amo ergo sum.

The light on her fades. The stage is black.

Figures enter from right and left, both Grey Figures and Sleepers but they are invisible. They carry strips of little lights in different shapes, like broken pieces of starry constellations, and, with them·, they make a very grand ballet of lights.

Chorus:
> one is one is one is one is one is one is one is one is one
> is one is one is one is one is one is one is one is one is
> (l'un est l'un est l'un est l'un est l'un est l'un est l'un)
> ivory pear (poire d'ivoire)
> one is one is one is one is one is one is one is one is one
> hoping to see (espoir de voir)
> one is one is one is one is one is one is one is one is one
> drinking hope (boire l'espoir)
> black glory (gloire noire)
> one is one is one is one is one is one is one is one is one
> believing hope (croire l'espoir)
> one is one is one is one is one is one is one is one is one
> seeing hope (voir l'espoir)
> one is one is one is one is one is one is one is one is one
> hoping for black (espoir de noir)
> one is one is one is one is one is one is one is one is one

The lights move in the dark as if the sky were dancing, clumps and dots and curves and lines of lights folding and spinning in and out of each other. They come together in a very tight clump of lights and then they wave out, and across the stage one can read the words, spelled out with lights:

MON DESIR

The lights come together again in a clump and again fan out, this time spelling out in little lights the words:

MONDE RIS

THE CITY OF NANTES (*raising her arms again*): I love, therefore I am. (J'aime, donc je suis.)

The lights begin to flow off the stage into the audience space…

Gamma-III

Gamma Fear

The GREY FIGURES carrying the strips of lights drift in the audience space. The SLEEPERS return to their beds still holding the lines and curves that glow with lights. The Beta rhythm of "One is one is one" changes to the slower Gamma rhythm of

> Is one one? is one one? is one one? is one one? is one one? is one one? is one one? is one one? is one one? is one one?

Over which the Sleepers are heard calling out.

SLEEPERS: Gamma! Come in, Gamma.

THE GREY FIGURES (*addressing the audience*): Is there danger of famine in your town?

SLEEPERS: Gamma! Come in, Gamma.

THE GREY FIGURES (*to the audience*): Is there enough corn in your bin?

SLEEPERS: Gamma, Gamma.

THE GREY FIGURES (*to the audience*): These are lean times.

SLEEPERS: Gamma.

THE GREY FIGURES (*to the audience*): Economy real bad.

SLEEPERS: Gamma.

THE GREY FIGURES (*to the audience*): Depression coming maybe; cycles of money.

SLEEPERS: Gamma, I'm afraid, Gamma.

THE GREY FIGURES (*to the audience*): Afraid are you?

SLEEPERS: Afraid, Gamma.

THE GREY FIGURES (*to the audience*): Afraid of my touch?

SLEEPERS: Afraid, Gamma.

THE GREY FIGURES (*to individual audience members. Intimate*): Afraid, if I touch you like this?

SLEEPERS: Afraid, Gamma.

THE GREY FIGURES (*each* GREY FIGURE, *always to a single spectator*): Afraid if I kiss you like this? (*They each lean in to kiss a spectator.*)

SLEEPERS: Afraid, Gamma.

The GREY FIGURES continue to go from spectator to spectator proffering touches and kisses. When there is a moment of hesitation or refusal on the part of the spectator, they murmur, "Afraid"—and flick off their lights and return to the stage space. When they hear an "Afraid," the SLEEPERS begin to turn off their lights also, and as the action continues, the voices of the SLEEPERS call out urgently as if looking for certainty in the encroaching dark.

SLEEPERS: Gamma! Gamma!

But when they turn out their lights they are silent. The scene ends in silence and darkness.

Delta-II

Imagine

Very dim light.

A Grey Figure crosses the stage with an immense burden. Suddenly the huge sack he's carrying bursts and stones spill all over the stage. The Sleepers roll out of their beds. Each begins to gather a few stones and to make music with them at the same time that they begin the strong hum of a Delta rhythm melody. Simultaneously two figures, grey, with flat (untoothed) rakes—like those used on gaming tables—rake the stones together, gathering the scattered pieces of the world. The chorus begins to repeat the word IMAGINE obsessively, and over this and the music of the stones being swept together and clacking, float the words of a song being sung by one of the Sleepers (Tom).

Song:

imagine the stars all drunk
with their tablets of twilight and truth
imagine a man's dark lips
and a woman's vessels of light
imagine the angel
with her thousand glittering hairs
imagine all the knowledge dreamers have
of the future with its unbroken pines
imagine the birds in the eyes
of the angels of wisdom
imagine the light
when love never loses
imagine the dialogue between yes and no
the loveliness of the questions and answers
imagine the thought
that unites day and night

imagine the thought
that unites one and two

Lights and sound dim out.

GAMMA–IV

BRISE MARINE

The melody of Delta gives way to the monotony of Gamma, and the figures crumble to the bottom of the sea and begin to roll back and forth regularly like watersoaked logs on the silty ocean floor. They roll forward counting slowly aloud:

1 2 3 4 5

and they roll backward, pulled by the undertow, like an object trapped in the motion of the sea, making .a droning marine sound.

CHORUS: 1 2 3 4 5 (*rolling forwards*)
                marine sound *(rolling backwards)*

Now ANTONIA's body, as she lies on her bed, begins to rise in the air drawn upwards by her belly as the CHORUS rolls forward, her head and feet remaining on pillow and on foot of bed. Then, as the CHORUS rolls backwards she sinks back flat. The CHORUS and ANTONIA alternate in dominating the sound.

ANTONIA:	to love to love to love to love to love
CHORUS:	1 2 3 4 5
ANTONIA:	without loss
CHORUS:	1 2 3 4 5
ANTONIA:	to love to love to love to love to love
CHORUS:	1 2 3 4 5
ANTONIA:	to love to love to love to love to love
CHORUS:	1 2 3 4 5
ANTONIA:	to flee! to flee down there!
CHORUS:	1 2 3 4 5
ANTONIA:	to love to love to love to love to love

CHORUS:	lost, without masts
ANTONIA:	to love to love to love to love to love
CHORUS:	1 2 3 4 5
ANTONIA:	to be inside the foam
CHORUS:	1 2 3 4 5
ANTONIA:	to love to love to love to love to love
CHORUS:	on the empty paper
ANTONIA:	to love to. love to love to love to love
CHORUS:	1 2 3 4 5
ANTONIA:	o my heart
CHORUS:	1 2 3 4 5
ANTONIA:	to love to love to love to love to love
CHORUS:	I'm leaving! steamer!
ANTONIA::	to love to love to love to love to love
CHORUS:	1 2 3 4 5
ANTONIA:	reconciled to death
CHORUS:	1 2 3 4 5
ANTONIA:	to love to love to love to love to love
CHORUS:	undertow

Blackout.

Beta-IV

The Unconscious Wish

The three female SLEEPERS—CATHÉRINE, ANTONIA and the CITY OF NANTES (ISHA)—form the figure of the Oracular Priestess on the central bed.

In front of them four GREY FIGURES form the Gates of the Unconscious. The SUPPLIANTS (the remaining SLEEPERS—TOM, CHRISTIAN, and HANON) lie stretched out on the floor to right and left in the foreground.

GATES OF THE UNCONSCIOUS CHORUS:
The Gates of the Unconscious are locked.
Who can loose the bolt?
Who can break the seal?

CHORUS OF SUPPLIANTS:
O Beta O Beta O Beta O Beta!

ORACLE:
I am here! Find me!
Unlock my mind!

SUPPLIANT (HANON): O Beta, how can I solve the enigma?

SUPPLIANT (CHRISTIAN): O Beta, how can I reconcile my teeth with love and ambition?

SUPPLIANT (TOM): O Beta, how can I not die?

The Gates open and the ORACLE speaks.

ORACLE (choral): Three women appear as the answers.

CATHÉRINE comes through the Gates surreptitiously, takes HANON's hand, and takes flight with him.

CATHÉRINE: The first woman is an expert in cracking safes.

The CITY OF NANTES comes drowsily to TOM and curls up and goes to sleep in his arms.

THE CITY OF NANTES: The second woman is asleep dreaming on the event.

ANTONIA comes to CHRISTIAN, pulls him up, and leads him forward, like Eurydice leading Orpheus; the Gates dissolve, and the people in it follow her.

ANTONIA: The third woman is moving with you, and if you look behind you will see that many follow with her.

Dimout.

Alpha-II
(Paradoxical Sleep—Rem Sleep—D-State)

"Act II"
The Plot Thickens

Order of the Dreams

1. Divine Defeats Dragnet (CATHÉRINE's dream)
2. The Eye of the Sheet (TOM's dream)
3. The Film Version of Prometheus (HANON's dream)
4. The Evolution of the Thumb (CHRISTIAN's dream)
5. Divine Shows Cathérine the Ropes (CATHÉRINE's dream)
6. Medea Temporizes (ANTONIA's dream)
7. Jail House Blues (CATHÉRINE's dream)
8. The Rat Maze (TOM's dream)
9. Prometheus Distributes Tracts (HANON's dream)
10. On the Waterfront (CATHÉRINE's dream)
11. The Upper and the Lower Worlds (HANON's dream)
12. Antonia's Dream (ANTONIA's dream)
13. The Cat Man (CHRISTIAN's dream)
14. The Beating of Wings (TOM's dream)
15. Orpheus Looks (ANTONIA's dream)
16. The Sleep of Prisoners (CATHÉRINE's dream)
17. The Death Lock (CHRISTIAN's dream)
18. The Oceanids (HANON's dream)
19. The Fish of Death (CATHÉRINE's dream)
20. The Magic Fire (TOM's dream)
21. Dante's Circles (TOM's dream)
22. Truth of the Womb (CHRISTIAN's dream)
23. Ocean Against Ocean (CATHÉRINE's dream)
24. What a Pleasure to Frighten Strangers (CATHÉRINE's dream)
25. Prometheus Sleeps (HANON's dream)
26. The Gun Kiss (CATHÉRINE's dream)

Alpha-II
Scene i

Divine Defeats Dragnet
(Cathérine's Dream)

A jagged rhythm.

Sleepers and Grey Figures move like the hunted, but their feet stay in place. Cathérine and Horacio slink between them. Two Grey Figure detectives prowl. They are on the hunt. They seize a woman. Identity check. She shows her papers to them. They release her. They stop Cathérine and Horacio.

Chorus: She has Trains of Thought.

Cathérine (*protesting, explaining, as the detectives put their hands on her*): But I'm an actress with the Living Theatre...

The Detectives begin to drag her away. The Grey Figure of Divine (Rain) slinks up. Intercedes. Embraces the officer. Kisses. Obscene gestures. Cathérine and Horacio escape onto the Train of Thought. Divine is opening the policemen's pants as the train departs.

Cathérine (*to Horacio as the railroad platform onto which they have climbed begins to move carrying them away to safety*): But who are you?

Horacio gives her a yellow dandelion he has been holding between his teeth.

Blackout.

Alpha-II
Scene 2

The Eye of the Sheet
(Tom's Dream)

Dragging a sheet from his bed, Tom moves with the Grey Figure of Ilion off the stage and into an aisle of the theatre. He selects a member of the public and speaks directly to this person.

Tom:
This play cannot be seen with two eyes.
You see this sheet?
You see this hole?
Is it a cigarette burn? A bullet hole?
It's the eye of a sheet. Look!
Do you know what a sheet is for?

Ilion:
To wrap up the mad.
To calm down lunatics when they get out of hand.

Tom and Ilion wrap up the spectator in the sheet.

Tom:
In psychiatric hospitals
this is what they do.

Ilion:
Now what is your wish?
To be free? Or to be sane?

Tom: Your wish is granted! (*They unwrap the spectator with a sweep.*) Pow!

Blackout.

Alpha-II
Scene 3

The Film Version of Prometheus
(Hanon's Dream)

The Grey Figure Ilion and several others stand on a bed like a camera crew. The bed becomes a dolly and one of the crew pushes it. Hanon lies on his bed. Two crew members raise the bed so that it stands straight up.

Grey Figure (Ilion):
Zoom in.
Dolly over to Prometheus.
Big close-up.
Now get a little of the rock.
Panorama of Caucasian peaks.
Desolation. Power and Force binding him to a rock.

The Grey Figures of Stephan and Horacio, making primitive sounds and moving with blunt, blind gestures, become Power and Force binding Prometheus (Hanon) to the bed/rock.

Grey Figure (Ilion):
Silence!
Camera. Sound. Go ahead, Hanon.

Chorus (*darkly*): You will forget your lines.

Hanon moves his mouth but no sound comes out.

Grey Figure (Ilion): Sound!

Grey Figure (Stephan) (*standing behind the rock*): Press very hard. I will be behind you. Press! Press!

Prometheus's bonds give. He moves forward, the Grey Figure of Stephan as Force behind him holding his arms out before him, the palms of his hands erect, a few centimeters from HANON's back, seeming to push him without touching him.

GREY FIGURE (ILION) (to *the crew, excited*): Keep turning!

HANON and STEPHAN move toward the audience space.

CHORUS: In place of his face, a rock.

Blackout.

Alpha-II
Scene 4

The Evolution of the Thumb
(Christian's Dream)

A woman, huddled over, bundled in cloth, arrives on the Train of Thought along with CHRISTIAN, who contemplates her as if gazing at the enigma of enigmas—Rodin's The Thinker or Rembrandt's Aristotle Contemplating the Bust of Homer.

There is a rumbling sound, like an impending earthquake. Panic positions as in Signorelli's End of the World. Everyone begins to topple, lose their balance. CHRISTIAN, however, remains unperturbed in meditation.

CONFUSED VOICES:
   What's that?
   Look! The chandelier!
   It's swinging!
   The water level!
   Get out of the building!
   Out of my way!
   Help!

CHRISTIAN (*pulling a hand out of the bundle*): LOOK!

Sudden and complete silence. The people look at him in wonder. CHRISTIAN holds the thumb of the hand between his own thumb and forefinger. He addresses the crowd like Mark Antony.

CHRISTIAN:
   Can this, the opposable thumb,
   dispel the disequilibrium
   in the community?
   The thumb is deliberate!

Who thought of it?

The people begin to regard their thumbs and the thumbs of the others with wonder, all holding them straight out before them on the end of their rigid extended arms. Great calm fills the air.

Blackout.

Alpha-II
Scene 5

Divine Shows Cathérine the Ropes
(Cathérine's Dream)

Everyone is rooted to the ground, as in Alpha-II, Scene 1, except the Grey Figure of Divine (Rain) and Cathérine, who move along the Train of Thought. Divine moves behind Cathérine, never touching her, but compelling her forward, as Stephan did with Hanon in Alpha-II, Scene 3, his arms extended, his palms erect.

Divine (Rain): Keep going straight ahead.

Cathérine: Divine, I...I...can't move.

They begin moving together in tandem, but all the time as if fighting a heavy counter-force.

Divine (Rain):
I'm pushing you. To the brink.
The police know everything, gaudy frogs.
Pissenlit...is...in...the slams...

Pissenlit (Horacio) appears behind them in the cage on the Train of Thought.
Blackout.

Alpha-II
Scene 6

Medea Temporizes
(Antonia's Dream)

The Train of Thought with HORACIO in the cage moves toward stage right pulling in its wake the divan with the sleeping CITY OF NANTES.

DIVINE (RAIN): Medea!

The rhythm of Umbanda breaks the former sound pattern. The GREY FIGURES begin to circle ANTONIA's bed chanting, all trancing out.

ANTONIA remains asleep. DIVINE dances up to her bed, his body shaking frenetically and seductively.

DIVINE:
Medea!
(ANTONIA *rises, responding to* DIVINE's *dance and invitation.*)
The ceremony of the perfect crime!
Love justifies everything!
I will stand beside you!
I will give you strength!
(*She begins to move, ecstatic, he behind her now, pushing without touching her.*)
Go through the wall!
The knife is the key!

ANTONIA climbs onto the Train of Thought. She raises her arms over the sleeping body of the CITY OF NANTES. She makes ecstatic sounds as she cuts the air with the sword.

ANTONIA: The sword of the Black Sea witch!

CHRISTIAN (*jumping onto the bed and dancing frenetically*):
Stronger, Antonia, and louder!

DIVINE (RAIN) (*breaking up the dance ceremony*):
STOP! The rehearsal is over for today.
Antonia will never learn the part.

ANTONIA collapses over the sleeping body of NANTES, who sleeps unperturbed.
Blackout.

Alpha-II
Scene 7

Jail House Blues
(Cathérine's Dream)

Everyone is lying down asleep, curling and uncurling on their beds and on the :floor. The City of Nantes on her couch is also very restless. Disturbed sleep.

Divine (Rain) (*Blues Song*):
Jail house mis'ry.
  Nothing nice to smell or see.
Locks and keys
  Nothing here for you and me.
Walls and rules
  Ay yai yai yai boo boo
Loveless school of death…

During the song, Cathérine rises stealthily and creeps to the cage on the Train of Thought where Horacio is locked up.

Cathérine: No one can see me. Invisible, like the people. I just have to move like a tree.

She opens the door to the cage. Enters. She and Horacio kiss. Loud noise of alarm bell as the cage with its door still swinging open moves out of sight.
Blackout.

Alpha-II
Scene 8

The Rat Maze
(Tom's Dream)

The people stand facing front like soldiers at attention, but they sway like palm trees. They make a crooning night sound. Their feet are again pasted to the ground. The CITY OF NANTES also stands and sways. SABUHL (ILION) and TOM crawl around on their bellies like rats.

TOM:
> We were crawling in back alleys like rats.
> This guy kept leading me through these streets.
> He seemed to know the way.
> I wasn't sure if he was taking me to my mother's house in
>   Connecticut
> or to—

SABUHL (ILION) (*turning back to him*): Sh!
> That name's unpronounceable!

> Blackout.

Alpha-II
Scene 9

Prometheus Distributes Tracts
(Hanon's Dream)

The crew is standing on the bed. STEPHAN directing.

STEPHAN:
Focus in on Prometheus
Scene 137. Prometheus distributing leaflets.
Action!

HANON:
Where are the props?

GREY FIGURE (MARIA NORA) (*whispering audibly*): We had to hide them... (*She goes to the sleeping figure of the* CITY OF NANTES *and begins to pull them out from under her. She goes on explaining herself.*) We didn't know where to put them. So I put them here. So at least we have them... You know what I mean. Hanon, how many do you want? Are these enough? (*She brings him a bunch of red and yellow and orange leaflets.*)

STEPHAN: Sound!

HANON (*to the audience*):
1. The human mind is free:
to dream whatever it wishes.
2. If the mind is free:
it is lawless.
3. The spirit rules action:
not from a throne.
(*He splashes the audience with the leaflets. Then, returning to the center of the stage area, speaks solemnly, like a hypnotist, moving his hands, mudras that have a mesmeric effect.*)
Everyone owns the night:

You write a play about the day within it;
The night is all yours:
You write a play about the day within it.

STEPHAN: Cut!

Blackout.

Alpha-II
Scene 10

On the Waterfront
(Cathérine's Dream)

All the characters of the waterfront—toughs, sailors, prostitutes, thieves, hustlers—all standing and gyrating their pelvic regions. DIVINE comes on leading CATHÉRINE and HORACIO.

DIVINE (*moving from one figure to the next, embracing, caressing, clutching, but leading* CATHÉRINE *and* HORACIO *all the time*): Slide like this. A slow ceremony with drums.
The virtue of the hard and the soft.
This one's a mute sailor.
Let me see your teeth.
Yes, they are the roses of Barcelona.
But under here...
(*He is crawling between* CHRISTIAN's *legs.*)
...a fisherman descends every evening into this blue house.

CATHÉRINE is embraced and kissed by a GREY FIGURE, HORACIO by ANTONIA, DIVINE and CHRISTIAN blend in a hot kiss.
Blackout.

Alpha-II
Scene 11

The Upper and the Lower Worlds
(Hanon's Dream)

Hanon (*to the public*):
Those leaflets—I need them back. They've got errata.
They should have been written like this:
(STEPHAN *hands him some paint and a brush, takes off his shirt, turns around exposing his back to the audience.*)
So:
(HANON *rubs the back sensually, then draws two lines.*)

The Upper World
and

The Lower World
meet.

(*He draws two big Xs between the lines.*)

Where? Where both worlds meet at a point:
in Solomon's Seal:

(*He completes the star.*)
the visible like the invisible:
the created like the as yet uncreated.

STEPHAN (*turning toward* HANON, *facing the public*):
Now the seal is invisible.
(*He extends his arms, spreads his legs, like Leonardo's proportionate
man.*)
But you see…
(*Everyone else repeats his movements.*)
…now I am the six points.

Blackout.

ALPHA-II
SCENE 12

ANTONIA'S DREAM
(ANTONIA'S DREAM)

HANON is conducting an exercise rehearsal. He is demonstrating movements which everyone does with him.

HANON:
Alpha   a wave like a scythe made of bat's teeth.
Beta   waves like the lips of a lake
Gamma   slow waves like the irregular emissions of
stars of first and second magnitude.
Delta   a dense throbbing, slowest of all, the deep
sleep of the mind...

ANTONIA: Julian!

HANON: Yes, Antonia?

ANTONIA: In the sleep play I would like to play Medea.

HANON:
This is the sleep play
and you are dreaming of playing Medea.
Blackout.

Alpha-II
Scene 13

The Cat Man
(Christian's Dream)

CHRISTIAN:
  Can we do the cat étude again?
  Yesterday there was something I wanted to point out.
  (*It is again like the Temple of the Cats.*)
  When the cats are asleep…
  Stretch. Hunch. Curl. Purr.

  CHRISTIAN walks among the cats. One of the cats transforms into a man. It is the GREY FIGURE who always plays the DOCTOR. He strokes CHRISTIAN affectionately, then swings him around and locks him in a half-nelson. All of the cats spring awake emitting terrified cries.
  Blackout.

Alpha-II
Scene 14

The Beating of Wings
(Tom's Dream)

Tom:

Suddenly the air was filled with the beating of wings.
(*The* Grey Figures *form a large bird which beats its wings and stamps its feet and surges menacingly toward* Tom.)
I felt myself pale.
I was pinned against a wall.
The bird was approaching me.
Standing over there was that professor—
pretending to smoke a cigarette.
I had this terrible sense of NO WAY OUT!
Sabuhl!

The Bird has almost descended on Tom. The Grey Figure of Sabuhl (Ilion) takes a sheet from a bed, wraps it around Tom's legs, takes his hand, and leads him forward.

Sabuhl: This way the bird will not know about your European roots.

The Bird: Not European. Not European. Not European…

The Bird changes direction, mumbling as it flies away. Blackout.

Alpha-II
Scene 15

Orpheus Looks
(Antonia's Dream)

Behind a sheet held by two GREY FIGURES, ANTONIA, invisible to the audience, walks led by CHRISTIAN as Orpheus. He has a lyre. As the sheet moves across the stage, TOM and DIVINE (RAIN) creep with it. ORPHEUS/CHRISTIAN beams long notes of music.

DIVINE: Can you see them?

TOM: I can see both of them. *She* can only see *him*. *He* can see no one.

ORPHEUS turns and looks at EURYDICE. DIVINE tears down the sheet.

DIVINE:
Look at me! Not him!
It will kill you! Look at me!
(ANTONIA *looks at* DIVINE.)
Life has many possibilities.

Blackout

Alpha-II
Scene 16

The Sleep of Prisoners
(Cathérine's Dream)

On the Train of Thought the CITY OF NANTES appears asleep in the cat cage. Walking along the railroad track come CATHÉRINE and HORACIO following the cage as it glides.

CATHÉRINE:
They are going to give her an injection.
It will appear as if there were no cause of death.

PISSENLIT (HORACIO):
Does she know she's asleep?

Blackout.

ALPHA-II
SCENE 17

THE DEATH LOCK
(CHRISTIAN'S DREAM)

CHRISTIAN is in the half-nelson he was in at the end of Scene 14. But it is a woman who holds him. He senses death at the back of his neck. HORACIO is in the same position, held also by a woman. Both struggle, then let go with a hair-raising sound and bound into the audience space.

Blackout.

Alpha-II
Scene 18

The Oceanids
(Hanon's Dream)

Everyone is standing in the Solomon's Seal position they were in at the end of Scene 11.

THE GREY FIGURE OF STEPHAN:
  This six-pointed position
  is the Artaudian double
  of the position of the person bound to the rock.
  (*To* HANON)
  Be a star!

HANON takes his position against the bed which the GREY FIGURES have raised to an upright position. They bind him to the bed/rock, the rope's lines mirroring the lines of the six-pointed star.

CHORUS:
  Seared by the sun gall, gnawed by night's cold teeth:
  He never sleeps,
  he howls.

HANON (*howling*):
  Tohu and Bohu
  Mind and clay
  Mind from eyes!
  Eppure si puo fare dall'acqua il fuoco!
  Nevertheless you can make fire out of water!

STEPHAN (*to the public*):
  Then the Oceanids come,
  the women of the sea, hydrogen and oxygen, that's you.

He begins to lead women from the public onto the stage, and as he does the chorus counts:

CHORUS:
Oceanid 1, Oceanid 1, Oceanid 1, etc.....
*(until someone begins to move toward the stage; at that moment
they add:)*
a pool
shwaaaaaaaa
of oxygen
(This continues in this way:)
Oceanid 2, Oceanid 2, Oceanid 2, etc ...
a lake
shwaaaaaaaa
water under wind...
Oceanid 3, etc....
water of fright
shwaaaaaaaa
stage fright
Oceanid 4, etc....
ocean people
shwaaaaaaaa
when you step on stage
Oceanid 5, etc....
river tank
shwaaaaaaaa
trembling of the heart

The public begins to come on stage and is arranged in
Oceanid positions around the feet of PROMETHEUS/HANON.
They are quickly led into swaying like waves and singing like
Debussy's sirènes. The GREY FIGURE OF STEPHAN swims from
the stage space toward the rear of the theatre.)

CHORUS
aha aha aha aha aha aha aha aha aha aha aha aha aha
range of silence
aha aha aha aha aha aha aha aha aha aha aha aha aha aha
silence silence silent seas

aha aha aha aha aha aha aha aha aha aha aha aha aha

HANON What silence?

STEPHAN (*from the back of the theatre*): Ours!

Blackout.

Alpha-II
Scene 19

The Fish of Death
(Tom's Dream)

Tom and Sabuhl (Ilion) push against the rock/bed as if it were a huge stone. Stage flooded with green-water light.

Sabuhl:
Push. Break the seal.
(*The bed/rock begins to turn.*)
It's guarded by that sleeping giant.
(*He indicates the public.*)

Tom (*indicating the Oceanids*): And all these people?

Sabuhl: Water babies.

A huge grey fish begins to stir menacingly. It is a group of Grey Figures mounted on a moving bed with a periscope rising vertically at its helm.

Tom (*scared*): And that?

Cathérine (*sprinting to* Tom's *side*): Fantomas! The Fish of Death! The Fish of Death!

Hanon (*speaking in his sleep from the bed/rock to which he's tied*): Tom!

Tom: What?

Hanon (*in his sleep still*): Trident missile.

Blackout.

ALPHA-II
SCENE 20

THE MAGIC FIRE
(TOM'S DREAM)

VOICE OF SABUHL (ILION) (*in the dark*): There are sparks: the other portions remain in total darkness. (*The lights change to flame.*)

TOM (*standing on a bed like an orchestra leader*):
The chorus creeps in
like the fingernails of fire.
All seated. Arms raised.
Trembling fingers.
Choral sound: ready?

CHORUS OF OCEANIDS:
Tsickatsickatsickatsicka
Tsickatsickatsickatsicka
Tsickatsickatsickatsicka

SABUHL: The bed/rock, please!

TOM:
Louder. Faster. Louder fast.
The flames obscure our visions.
Now: *she* enters,
She who has disobeyed her father.

The CITY OF NANTES, helmeted, with spear, shield, and cloak, standing beside a stage rock, in the heroic pose of Brunhilde, glides in on the Train of Thought. SABUHL cloaks and helmets TOM as Wotan, who then ascends the Train of Thought. TOM and the CITY OF NANTES beam loud notes of sound. The fire sound of the CHORUS rises and emits steaming hisses at its climaxes amidst its crackles. The music of the finale of Wagner's Die Walküre soars. Magic Fire music.

Wotan and Brunhilde entwine. She sinks into sleep on the stage rock. Darkness encircles all but the ring of fire around the bed/rock and the sleeping CITY.

Blackout.

Dante's Circles
(Tom's Dream)

The Magic Fire continues. Tom leaps from the Train into the fire, and squirms like a figure lapped by flames in a Dantesque vision.

Tom:
    It was like a postcard
    inserted into my dream
    I leapt into the flames
    Flames up to the waist
    Hot coals on genitals
    A Dante circle writhing with homosexuals

    The Doctor comes in riding on the Train of Thought.

The Doctor
    Anyone who has ever had any homosexual experience—
    cat or dog—or even a fantasy—you!—
    you! you! I know who you are!
    you!

    Still menacing the audience, he disappears.
    Blackout.

ALPHA-II
SCENE 22

TRUTH OF THE WOMB
(CHRISTIAN'S DREAM)

The Fish of Death is moving through the water.

CHRISTIAN (*instructing those who are floundering in the water being pursued by the Fish*):
Push. Puuuuuuuuush through the water.
Puuuuuuuuuuuuuuuuush.
(*As he speaks he arranges the audience members who have come on stage as swimmers. On one side the Fish of Death; on the other, the swimmers; the two groups undulating back and forth confronting each other.*)
A child is light…nine months of atoms…
molecules, atoms, amulets made of nipple…

THE GREY FIGURE OF HENRIETTE (*swimming beside him*):
Nine months of atoms:
Truth of the womb
against the lie of the hull…

Blackout.

Alpha-II
Scene 23

Ocean Against Ocean
(Cathérine's Dream)

Green light. Fish of Death. Everyone swimming.

Fish of Death Chorus:
Depth 400 meters:
Sound bladder adjacent:
Consumption constant:
Enemy in close range.

Cathérine (*going from one* Oceanid *to another*):
They are planning to kill us.
(*Indicating* Prometheus):
They will begin with him.
Then they will get Pissenlit;
They will get Divine, and Sabuhl, and me.
They will get you.

The Oceanids back up against the advance of the Fish of Death.
Blackout.

Alpha-II
Scene 24

What a Pleasure to Frighten Strangers
(Cathérine's Dream)

The Grey Figure of Pissenlit (Horacio) stands in front of Prometheus, bound and asleep in his upright bed. He has a clap-board.

Pissenlit:
  CIAC!
  (*He speaks through a megaphone.*)
  Oceanids, on the ground over there—
  arms outstretched. Show them how. That's it.
  The sound is this:
    What a pleasure to frighten strangers.
  Repeat:
    What a pleasure to frighten strangers.

Chorus:
    What a pleasure to frighten strangers.

Pissenlit:
  Now, Cathérine...piccoli passi, piccoli passi...

Cathérine begins with extravagant gestures to unbind Prometheus.

Cathérine: "Prometheus Unbound," Take One!

Pissenlit: CIAC!

Blackout.

Alpha-II
Scene 25

Prometheus Sleeps
(Hanon's Dream)

Pissenlit:
CIAC!
Closeup of Prometheus sleeping.

Light on Prometheus only. He curls and uncurls. Pissenlit
hands him a beaker.

Hanon:
Drink,
Pass the beaker from mouth to mouth.
Drink the whole,
Drink the ocean.
13 measures draws out the scroll.

Blackout.

ALPHA-II
SCENE 26

THE GUN KISS
(CATHÉRINE'S DREAM)

DIVINE (RAIN), CATHÉRINE, and ANTONIA plunge into the audience, charge down the aisle. DIVINE selects a spectator, addresses him/her accusingly while CATHÉRINE aims a pistol at his/her head, ANTONIA standing helplessly by, flapping.

DIVINE:
  You!
  Your crimes are your purple! Your people!
  You jammed your emeralds into me, fishhooks.

CATHÉRINE:
  And the guillotine is still cutting heads off
  in your mind!

DIVINE (*shaking his head, dissenting*):
  No corks, no crops, no rivers kiss that way.

He sinks to the ground burying her gun in his hand as he fades.
  ANTONIA kisses the stranger.
  Blackout.

ALPHA-II
SCENE 27

LOST IN AN IMPENETRABLE FOREST
(CITY OF NANTES'S DREAM)

The glass box containing the CITY OF NANTES slides in on the Train of Thought. She is looking out of the side as if it were the windeow of a train and as if she were straining to see where she is. Railroad sounds.

VOICE: Nous arrivons à la ville de Nantes. Arrêt trois minutes. Nantes. Le Corail. Le train 352 part à 15 heures 13. Le train 452 a du être retardé de 5 heures, cause des inondations. Nantes. Arrêt trois minutes.

The CITY OF NANTES gets out of her glass box, descends from the train, walks among the sleeping Oceanids, awakes one of them, to whom she speaks in panic.

THE CITY OF NANTES: My street! Do you know the address?

Blackout.

ALPHA-II
SCENE 28

SHE
(ANTONIA'S DREAM)

A sound of wind, storm. Snow falls. THE CITY OF NANTES
leads ANTONIA, who leads PISSENLIT (HORACIO) and others
over bed-mountains. They are travelers in the Himalayas.
SHE (HELGA) wears an elaborate headdress and stands in the
center singing.

SHE (HELGA): Youth!

ANTONIA: How old is she?

NANTES: She is Mother of Stone and Water.

SHE: I lived before wind came.

AMUH (MINA): How beautiful.

PISSENLIT (HORACIO): Her f ace is a mask covering old Vienna.

ANTONIA (*addressing* SHE): What is your secret?

SHE: I bathe in eternity!
   (*She sings mad notes of music.*)
   Ahahahahahahahahahahabahaaaaaaaaaaaaaaaaa

ANTONIA (awed): Who is she?

NANTES: She is She.

ANTONIA: And you?

NANTES: Ahabahahabahahahahaaaaaaaa

ANTONIA: How old are you?

NANTES: One thousand nine hundred and sixty seven.

   The CITY OF NANTES sinks to sleep on ANTONIA's bed.
   Blackout.

Alpha-II
Scene 29

Pandora's Box
(Christian's Dream)

The Grey Figure of Henriette as Pandora tramps in on the Train of Thought.

PANDORA: (to Christian):
Mmmmmmmmmmmm?
How long are you going to forget me? Hmmmmmmmm?
(*To everyone.*)
How long?
You don't remember me, no?
I came to get my things. I'm going.
(*To* Stephan.)
You don't remember me?
Put your hand on my breast. Then you will remember.
(*To* Hanon.)
You don't remember either?

HANON: Pandora?

PANDORA:
Yes. I came to get my things.
My ten thousand scattered things.
(*She goes to* Antonia's *bed, where the* City of Nantes *lies sleeping, wakes her, takes hold of her, and walks with her toward the glass box on the Train of Thought.*)
She belongs in my box.
Everything lost and kicked around.
I'm picking up the pieces.
I'm protecting hope from your cheap obliteration.
Come, I'm gathering my things.
She belongs in my box.

The City of Nantes enters the glass box and goes to sleep. Pandora closes the box.

Blackout.

Alpha-II
Scene 30

The Beach at Pornic
(Christian's Dream)

Little boats sail across the Train of Thought. The City of Nantes is asleep in her glass box.

Christian: I once dreamt of a woman with golden hair. who was talking to my sister while showing her some embroidery.

Grey Figure (Stephan): Would everybody stretch out on the sand? Nicolas! We need a sad lighting for this scene. A melancholy sun.

Christian (*walking from woman to woman*): She seemed very familiar to me... I thought I had seen her often before...

Grey Figure (Stephan) (*to the public*): Appear relaxed. Take off your clothes, leaving just your undergarments—like bathing suits.

Christian: I thought I had seen her very often before. Her face was clear to me but I was unable to recognize her.

Grey Figure (Stephan): Natural. Are you ready, Hanon? (Hanon *remains immobile*.)

Christian: Then I went to sleep once more and the dream-picture was repeated. But in this second dream I spoke to the fair-haired lady and asked her if I had not had the pleasure of meeting her somewhere before. To which she replied:

The Grey Figure of Henriette: Of course, don't you remember the plage at Pornic?

SODIUM LIGHT ! ! ! Sounds of insanity. NO blackout.

ALPHA-II
SCENE 31

PANDEMONIUM

SODIUM LIGHT. Sound of insanity.

The DOCTOR appears on the Train of Thought. He holds some kind of sparkler device in his hand like a ray gun shooting off sparks.

CATS howling and scatting about in terror.

The CITY OF NANTES twisting and turning in her glass box in nightmare sleep.

CHRISTIAN (*to the public*): THE AUDIENCE SHOULD ALSO BE HOWLING LIKE CATS! HOWL!

CATHÉRINE (*screaming, tearing the ropes off* HANON): The chains! The books! (*Gunshot. Machine gun fire.*)

PISSENLIT (HORACIO) (*falling at* CATHÉRINE'*s feet, shot*): Lorca!

HANON (*freed from the bed/rock*): I got out of bed...and I saw... that everyone was...dying! (*People and cats are collapsing everywhere, writhing.*)

TOM: Oh, god!

GREY FIGURE OF STEPHAN: Torches!

The CITY OF NANTES (*sitting up in the glass box*): LIGHTS! LIGHTS!

Blackout.

BETA–V

I HAVE A WISH

GREY FIGURES of miners, wearing miners' hats with lights, chip softly with muffled picks under the tracks of the Train of Thought. They are accompanied by the audience members who became first involved in the dreams as Oceanids. The sound of the chipping grows disturbingly in the course of the scene.

The CITY OF NANTES with her eyes open, listening, slides into view lying on her belly on the divan, watched over by a GREY FIGURE wrapped in black, like an image created by Gauguin.

The five SLEEPERS have collapsed in their beds.

Their grey doubles lie under the beds, where faint lights illuminate them.

The five GREY FIGURES are lying on their backs under the beds, their bodies undulating in slow waves as if they were trying to send some kind of message, wordless, into the SLEEPERS' bodies.

The SLEEPERS tap on the beds, lift the mattresses, as if trying to reach a prisoner in another cell in the tier downstairs. They tap with a certain urgency, they call softly, not a whisper, but with the emotional content of need.

CHRISTIAN:
(*Knocking, knocking, knocking.*)
I have a wish.
(*Knocking, knocking, more desperately.*)
I have a wish!
(*Knocking.*)
Can you hear me?
(*Knock, knock.*)

HANON: There's something greater than earth or sky... Can

you hear? Something greater than even lymph or eyes…
The void is nothing.
(*Knock, knock.*)

Tom: Listen…the void is nothing…

Antonia: Not unlikely that his body be separated from his mind…
(*Knock, knock.*)
What's love for?
(*Knock knock.*)

Cathérine:
(*Knock knock.*)
If the seven cannot hear, who can hear?…
(*Knock knock.*)
If it's iron, can't it turn to fruit?

The City of Nantes (*suddenly, as if waking up during a nightmare, crying out*): Amuh, stop that knocking!

Amuh (one of the miners, chipping away): Stops when you want it to.

Brief silence. The City of Nantes smiles and sighs and falls back relaxed as do all of the other Sleepers. The knocking of the miners resumes. The Grey Figures begin to slide out from under the beds and to embrace the Sleepers, speaking as they do.

Tom's Grey Figure (Ilion) (*to* Tom): The void? Drink the wine from between my lips.

Hanon's Grey Figure (Stephan) (*to* Hanon): Something greater? Death is only a gangster, yes.

Christian's Grey Figure (Henriette) (*to* Christian): A wish? Desire, each letter of it, a rung on the only ladder.

Cathérine's Grey Figure (Horacio) (*to* Cathérine): Iron and fruit? Everything meets on the road of words, parts on the road of self.

The miners' knocking and chipping stops. The miners curl up and go to sleep. Intense silence.

THE CITY OF NANTES (*with understanding*): When I want it to stop...

Soft music, ten seconds...everyone contentedly sleeping. Blackout.

GAMMA–V

GAMMA RESTRAINT

Gamma wave rises, punctuated with deep menacing marks. Sound grows rapidly more frightening.

HANON, TOM, and CHRISTIAN dress the GREY FIGURE OF STEPHAN ceremonially in a straitjacket. The public inspects the locks.

The drumming becomes more insistent.

A gun arrives on a violet cushion on the Train of Thought. CATHÉRINE takes it, walks around with the cushion and the gun, showing it to people in the audience and to the sleeping ANTONIA.

Two CATS in glowing collars crawl along the Train of Thought.

STEPHAN rolls on the floor of the stage struggling to get out of the straitjacket.

Blackout.

Delta-III

Meditation on Primitive Mysteries

Semi-Chorus I (Sleepers): Murder!

Semi-Chorus II (Grey Figures): No! (*Incredulous*)

Semi-Chorus I (Sleepers): Yes!

Semi-Chorus II (Grey Figures): No! (*Still incredulous.*)

Semi-Chorus I (Sleepers): Yes! Murder!

Semi-Chorus II (Grey Figures): Who?

Semi-Chorus I (Sleepers): THE DOG!

The City of Nantes (*mumbling*): My dog!...

Grey Figure of Horacio (*sitting on the side of the bed, then rising*):
An amiable dog, centered on friendship.
But rather than recount the story,
I ask you to act it out.
All those here, on this side of the stage:
each of you be this dog.
He was a performing dog and stood often on his hind legs.
Haven't you dreamt at some time or other of yourself as an
    animal representing your own animal nature?
But you must only enjoy each other
and no comic details
because this dog never played for laughs.
(*The performers aid the public on stage right in assuming the
physical characteristics and postures of a canine étude. Each is given
a dark brown glove with a tooth at the end of each finger to wear.*)
And that day, in a tree outside the house,
I noticed again the squirrel—
all of you on stage left—be this squirrel—
this squirrel whom I have always enjoyed observing

286

because of the arabesques of his body
his capacity to leap from branch to branch
a kind of mammalian grasshopper in flight—
(*The performers aid the public in assuming the emblematic posture
of a squirrel. Each is given a tail-like curl to hold.*)
The dog sees the· squirrel!—
And like an arrow shot from some neolithic bow drawn
taut in his spine
WHAM!
He shoots himself like an arrow into the back of this
other smaller creature.
(*The dogs leap upon the squirrels, seizing them by the middle,
twirling them around, twisting them to the ground, wrenching the
squirrel tails from them with their tooth claws.*)
We ran out of the house. Isha!
(*The* CITY OF NANTES *comes running to help, furiously pulling
the dogs away from the squirrels.*)
We grabbed at the dog and pulled him away from the
squirrel
who lay on the ground shivering with death.

ILION (*rising and speaking to a spectator-dog*): What did you feel
in your body just now, when it jerked and pounced?

MARIA NORA (*to another spectator-dog*): Some kind of pleasure—
like an absent thought?

A funerary hum. The people—dogs and squirrels and
spectator-guests—slowly leave the scene, placing a squirrel
tail on each of the SLEEPERS, like a rose placed on a grave. Five
of the spectators are instructed by the GREY FIGURES to take
their places under the beds.

STEPHAN (*still rolling on the ground in the straitjacket*):
Dark desires, then,
are they fragments of the great mosaic
of our divine unity with nature?

HORACIO (*as he walks off with the* CITY OF NANTES, *comforting her*): We buried the dead squirrel...

TOM: ...noting the peaceful look on his face...

RAIN (*as squirrel*):
The dead squirrel rises.
What is left is the memory of it,
The light of it in motion,
Its spirit now resident
In the fluid archives of our minds.

The five SLEEPERS rise and, standing on their beds holding the squirrel tails like peace-denoting palm leaves, sing.

CHORUS:
The divine unity of nature:
must we say that we share as well
the limitations of pigs and fishes?
Of Wolf the Hunter?
Of Great Eagle that eats rats?

Dim-out.

Gamma-VI

War

Three or four women, naked, are standing on a sliding platform which is pulled slowly backwards across the Train of Thought. The women themselves stand in a frieze, motionless. As they reach stage right, spears, machine guns, shields, and Roman helmets held and worn by otherwise naked men begin to appear on extreme stage left. Frieze, two seconds. Hommage to Picasso's Massacre in Korea.

Blackout.

Beta-VI

And Peace

Lights up again on the Train of Thought. The same image seen at the end of Gamma-VI, the naked women, the armed men.

The women begin to walk slowly toward the motionless spears. The CHORUS sings, melodically and allegro. SEMI-CHORUS I consists of the SLEEPERS, SEMI-CHORUS II of the women.

SEMI-CHORUS I:
    Land Mass
    Foundation
    Glory

SEMI-CHORUS II:
    The body...

SEMI-CHORUS I:
    Triumph
    Beauty
    Understanding...

SEMI-CHORUS II:
    ...is the phenomenal form...

SEMI-CHORUS I:
    Wisdom
    Crown

SEMI-CHORUS II:
    ...of the will to live.

SEMI-CHORUS I:
    Endless

As the women cross the lights dim to blackout.

Alpha-III
(Paradoxical Sleep—Rem Sleep—D-State)

"Act III"
The Great Sleep Rehearsal
(Everyone's Dream)

A roaring, crackling, irregular sound. The conversation and movements are all super-rapid.

CHRISTIAN (*in the dark*): Places! Places! Please!

Strong lights on. The women and men who were naked in the preceding scene are dressing. The sleeping CITY OF NANTES slides into view on her couch.

CATHÉRINE (*walking into the audience space*): I don't understand. I'm not on stage? I'm sitting in the audience?

HORACIO: Yes, like part of the people.

ANTONIA (*waking in panic*): Judith! Judith! What am I doing in this scene?

CATHÉRINE: Go onto the Train of Thought. You are in the position of a servant.

ANTONIA: Whose servant?

RAIN: Love's servant.

HANON: Can we put all details aside and concentrate on the mass?

CHRISTIAN: Can we take places for the Great Alpha Scene! Everybody!
First there are five people in the beds...
(*He begins to select people from the audience.*)
You—you—you— Stop! When you are asleep you walk like this:
(*He walks bent over, dragging his hands.*)

A prehistoric sleep.

TOM: Is Tom anywhere?

ILION: I'm over here.

TOM: Shall we show the Mastodon Walk? Look, like this, dragging the hands, till you come to your place and slide into sleep...

CHRISTIAN: You—you—would you go into that bed over there—in the center, yes. Remember you are very tired. You must pass through the Gates of Alpha. It's a form of auto-hypnosis, going to sleep. Good. More sleepers. This is everyone's secret life. Ah, but what is the secret? Sleep... Now the five doubles for them, please—also with them— you and you and you and you and you, please...and another ten or twenty sleepers here on stage, lying down... (*His voice gets rubbery.*)

RAIN (*talking to himself*): Rain, you should put on the trans-vestite gown now and stand next to the other servant.

HANON: Can we do the trance first? I think we can do it with a sound.

CATHÉRINE: It's too messy. Sleep is a cycle. A smooth revolu-tion.
(*With* HORACIO's *help she stands on one of the seats in the audience and faces the people.*)
Every time you sleep—and surely when you dream—you are revolting against the programme of the day!

HORACIO: But the body is in repose. Vulnerable. Passive. A container of trust. Try it.

STEPHAN: Could everyone try that? Just a relaxed swaying back and forth...

The audience begins to sway back and. forth.

HANON: Humming... So... (*He establishes a hum among the*

audience.) Julian!

STEPHAN: Yes?

HANON: What did you want here?

STEPHAN: A Utopian rite.

HANON: How is that? What is the order?

STEPHAN: The ritual goes like this.
In the dream there is a fusion of thoughts
of which we make a masque here on stage
among the sleeping people, in this room all full of them.
The dream contains a wish of some kind. And a negation.
And a resolution. So much for that.

HANON: When the emblems of the drama stir the poetry within you, then, in the trance of the Alpha rhythm you rise from from your seat—if you wish—and like the molecules of the sea we move with each other in solemn flow, pulling out of the reserves of the mind movements we have never in our waking lives performed alone or with one another.

In the stage space, three dramas have begun:
A tombstone appears on the Train of Thought. Three mourners in black place it at the head of the bed of one of the spectator-sleepers. The mourners weep—in the manner of an Elizabethan masque—and one of them crouches at the foot of the bed, climbs over it, and raises the spectator-sleeper up and into movement, a ritual which is repeated at two or three other beds.

Two people, near the proscenium line, attack each other brutally with stiffened gestures like mechanical toys, repeating and repeating the same movements like bedevilled dolls locked in the workings of a machine set in perpetual motion.

ANTONIA, pursued by a man in a white jacket, flees down the aisle of the theatre while RAIN, in transvestite gown. is chased by a man up the other aisle; and all the while the whole theatre is being coaxed into motion.

The whole theatre is moving back and forth like the waves of the sea, everyone has become an Oceanid, the sound that is being made is like that of the sirènes, but the GREY FIGURE OF THE DOCTOR, appearing, succeeds in censoring the desire to 1) continue the sounds and the movements and 2) defy his attempt to interrupt the rite. When the public has been restored to its conventions, he continues.

THE GREY FIGURE OF THE DOCTOR: Attention! Attention, please! Stephan! Maria! Kommt her! (STEPHAN *is freed from the straitjacket at this moment if he has not yet freed himself.*) Now, this cat—Stephan—we are placing on a stone surrounded by water... (*He moves with the two* CATS *onto the Train of Thought much as he did in Scene 2.*) When he relaxes into Paradoxical Sliep, he will fall into the water. He has been on this stone for seventy-two days now and is severely deprived of REM Sleep. This cat does not dream. Attention, please! And this one—Maria—whenever she enters Delta or Thinking Sleep—we give her an electric shock. She is one hundred percent deprived of Deep Sleep, and after some weeks we see that she is dead. It is clear what that proves. (MARIA-CAT *slumps down dead.*) The other cat, however, dream-deprived, you see, begins to go mad. He sees phantoms, he sees imaginary food, nonexistent prey, goes through strange contortions, very uncatlike, and will even mount and fuck a dead cat— (STEPHAN AS CAT *mounts and begins to make love to the dead* MARIA-CAT.) —something unprecedented in the animal world. So you see. (THE DOCTOR *now begins to apply electrodes to the sleeping* CITY OF NANTES.) Momentum for the dream cycle comes from the lower part of the brain, but the elaboration, the refinements, the brilliance and the nuance, the art comes from the cortex... Ah, what has happened to the tom? (*He walks over; the* STEPHAN-CAT *is also dead. Walking back to the* CITY OF NANTES) Now, let us see what is happening here. (*Loud buzz.* NANTES *sits up, confused.*) What were you dreaming? (NANTES *shakes her head in confusion and falls back to sleep.*) O.K. Get rid of the cats.

The performers put the dead cats in wheelbarrows and roll them up the aisles of the theatre, like garbage, and out.

The stage lights go down.

The house lights come up.

The dream dissolves.

STIR UP MY PASSION
by Ilion Troya

The Archaeology of Sleep, Julian Beck's testament as a poet, springs from an interest in the subject of sleep that he and Judith Malina shared throughout their lives together with The Living Theatre. They recognized the importance of sleep, considering we humans spend one-third of our lives in slumber. Is there more to it than rest and silence?

Judith, always seeking to better understand her own difficulty with uninterrupted sleep, collected articles on the scientific research. Julian tried to sleep one hour less every night, gaining more time to be alert and creative. Sleep was not a given for them, it was a quest. In 1983, research on sleep was a new field, pioneered by the Stanford University Sleep Research Center, inaugurated thirteen years before. The study changed their concepts, engaged the company, and resounded well with the artists and cultural activists we met in France.

The Living Theatre's production of a new play on the subject of sleep was subsidized by the new socialist government of François Mitterrand and welcomed by the socialist Maison de la Culture of Nantes, a rival of the older, conservative culture center of the city. The Living Theatre was called in to stir things up and awaken some real-life enthusiasm to begin a new progressive public administration.

The Archaeology of Sleep began as research by the company, each in their own language: English, Italian, French, German, Spanish, Portuguese. From our different cultural perspectives, we all had something to share. Lodged in Tharon Plage, a nearby beach resort, in the dead of winter, the company enjoyed the opportunity of living together as a collective of thirty artists under the same roof, with ample rehearsal space to work on the new play, which would be translated into

French for the Nantes performances.

As the project gained momentum, Julian conducted one-on-one interviews with each member of the company. Personal details, including embarrassing or queasy moments, actual dream recollections, subject matter that seemed germane to the play's leitmotif, enriched the play with each one's personal confessions and thoughts.

Together, we undertook planned experiments such as attempts to induce collective dreams, choosing an uncommon in-common experience to dream about; improvising a maze with furniture, fabric, and colored lights for all to go through; and filming the actors in their sleep. With the artists, authors, students, and activists of Nantes, we collaborated on the Museum of Sleep project, a series of performances and events, readings, and film viewings at the Maison de la Culture, which happened for a week while the play opened and was playing at Salle Paul Fort in May 1983.

The title came from a book Judith Malina and Hanon Reznikov were reading, Michel Foucault's *The Archaeology of Knowledge*, a method to analyze the systems of thought and knowledge as discursive enunciates which follow rules lying beneath consciousness. Their conversations about Foucault's method furthered Julian Beck's concept for a play dealing with the conscious and unconscious mind's limits of verbal expression and thought at each phase of sleep, depicted on the stage from the threshold of consciousness to the successive phases of brain waves, depth, thought, fear, and dreams, a repeated cycle in the course of a night's sleep in a ninety-minutes experiential play.

It could be read as a nonsensical surreal poem, but the play is not as abstract as it seems. There is more to it. Each actor embodies several characters, including their own selves, with set pairings and interactions between actors. And the audience space is constantly sweetly invaded by the actors. Several moments of I and Thou (in the Martin Buber sense) are played out with individual audience members, including soft and steady touch, an attempt to communicate in pregnant silence, an interpersonal, surprising, pleasant or discomfiting experience. Is theatre different from life? Are we aware of our fear of each other?

Deep inside the play, Antonia dreams she is playing Medea; by the end she is Antonia singing of love. Isha turns into Miss New York, then the Queen of Spades with Ilion as the King of Spades, then a Valkyrie with Tom as Wotan. Tom becomes obsessed with his European roots when his shadow, Sabuhl, attempts to save him from the Rock Bird. And then there is the "tom" in the cage and the lab cats, much used in sleep research as they are particularly sleepy animals. This brings in the ethical, moral question of research on animals. Out of a dream comes wildlife and an epic on the crucial question of killing animals. Gigi's sweet dog Shrimsley killed a squirrel in our garden in Tharon Plage. The vegetarian community absolved the culprit on the grounds it was merely instinctual, no malice or profit. And the question was raised: can humans do better than being instinctual? Able to abstain from killing?

All of a sudden, in an aisle: "This is the sheet's eye!" Smoking in bed? Dangerous! Somnambulism, *La Sonnambula*. Confusing dreams and word-twisting. The lovely character of Pissenlit (piss-on-bed, dandelion in French). Chance games and Mallarmé. Fragments of research on sleep fluctuating, flotsam and jetsam between the shores of memory and dream, in search of freedom sleep provides. The perennial quest of The Living Theatre for language, since the beginning with Gertrude Stein, always revisiting its poetical and theatrical roots, Jean Cocteau to Jackson McLow and John Cage. Julian Beck's constant writing and re-writing of flaming poetry, *Songs of the Revolution*, his broader sense of language as an instrument for social change, inseparably with Judith, a poet and playwright of her own and the director of most Living Theatre plays including *Sleep*.

Audience members are invited to come onto the stage during the play's climax and lie down with the actors on oversized beds. The dim lights, the music, the words entice Morpheus to seduce nearly all. Then, with a sudden wash of lights and sound, the actors rise, the audience members awake, and there they are, taking a bow.

At the beginning of 1983, when Julian interviewed me in Tharon Plage, he asked me what seemed important to include in the play. I remember mentioning "a sense of mystery-solving" and "the fear-of-death aspect of sleep." This was before the diagnosis of his cancer; and after, it made even deeper sense to me. Apart from a Jewish tombstone that slides by on the background "train-of-thought" track device, there is no direct mention of his Damocles' sword in the play, but, oh, how he howls against the useless death that is preventable and must be stopped! We got closer together, Julian and I, those days and after, when the passion turned into compassion, and we followed the path together for two more years. He was most productive then. Now that for me he's mostly thought, and my thoughts are in him and Judith, I keep translating his and her words into Brazilian books. It would be nostalgic if their works did not still stir up my passion.